Illu

1. A Scene from *The Beggar's Opera*. By William Hogarth, 1729. (Lavinia Fenton kneels on the right. Her future husband, the Duke of Bolton, watches from the far right.)
2. Miss Kitty Fisher as *Cleopatra Dissolving the Pearl*. By Edward Fisher, after Sir Joshua Reynolds, c.1752–1763.
3. Maria, Countess of Coventry. By Gavin Hamilton, 1753.
4. Mrs Horton, later Viscountess Maynard. By Sir Joshua Reynolds, c.1767–69.
5. *The Third Duke of Grafton Divorcing His First Wife*. By Anonymous, 1769.
6. Lady Elizabeth Stanley, Countess of Derby. By Sir George Romney, 1776–78.
7. Elizabeth Chudleigh, the Duchess of Kingston. By Anonymous (undated).
8. The Ladies of Llangollen. By J.H. Lynch, after Mary Parker, 1828.
9. *Florizel and Perdita*. By Anonymous, 1783. (George IV and Mary Robinson are shown as one person.)
10. William Beckford. By Francesco Bartolozzi, 1772.
11. Emma, Lady Hamilton. By John Jones, after Sir George Romney, 1785.
12. *The Disconsolate Sailor*. By Charles Williams Argus, 1811. (Catherine Tylney-Long chooses William Wellesley-Pole over the Duke of Clarence.)
13. *Lady Caroline Lamb in Her Page's Dress*. By Anonymous (undated).
14. Memorial Portrait of Lord Byron. By Mathieu Barathier, 1826.
15. Marguerite, Countess of Blessington. By Sir Thomas Lawrence, 1822.
16. *The Rat Catcher*. By Henry Heath, 1825. (The Duke of Wellington and Harriette Wilson discuss her memoirs.)

Credits

Plates 1, 2, 10, 11, 16: Courtesy of the Yale Center for British Art; public domain.

Plates 3, 15: Courtesy of Project Gutenberg; public domain.

Plate 4: Courtesy of the Metropolitan Museum of Art; public domain.

Plates 5, 6, 8: Courtesy of the Wellcome Collection; public domain.

Plates 7, 13: Courtesy of the Internet Archive; public domain.

Plate 9: Courtesy of the Library of Congress Prints and Photographs Division; public domain.

Plate 12: Courtesy of the Art Institute of Chicago; public domain.

Plate 14: Courtesy of the Rijksmuseum; public domain.

This Book belongs to;
Elvana Wongan
Phone; 07738 428244
email; erhw22@gmail.com

The Real Bridgerton

The Real Bridgerton

Catherine Curzon

PEN & SWORD HISTORY

First published in Great Britain in 2023 by
Pen & Sword History
An imprint of
Pen & Sword Books Ltd
Yorkshire – Philadelphia

ISBN 978 1 39908 240 2

A CIP catalogue record for this book is
available from the British Library.

Typeset by Mac Style
Printed and bound in the UK by CPI Group (UK) Ltd,
Croydon, CR0 4YY.

Pen & Sword Books Limited incorporates the imprints of Atlas,
Archaeology, Aviation, Discovery, Family History, Fiction, History,
Maritime, Military, Military Classics, Politics, Select, Transport,
True Crime, Air World, Frontline Publishing, Leo Cooper, Remember
When, Seaforth Publishing, The Praetorian Press, Wharncliffe
Local History, Wharncliffe Transport, Wharncliffe True Crime
and White Owl.

For a complete list of Pen & Sword titles please contact

PEN & SWORD BOOKS LIMITED
47 Church Street, Barnsley, South Yorkshire, S70 2AS, England
E-mail: enquiries@pen-and-sword.co.uk
Website: www.pen-and-sword.co.uk

Or

PEN AND SWORD BOOKS
1950 Lawrence Rd, Havertown, PA 19083, USA
E-mail: Uspen-and-sword@casematepublishers.com
Website: www.penandswordbooks.com

To the shamelessly scandalous...
and those who keep it under their hats.

Contents

Acknowledgements

In one of the strangest years of all, the most marvellous people of all are more precious than ever. Kathryn and Rob, what would I do without you? And Jon, Laura, and Michelle… you truly deserve all the cakes. Or chips. As for you, Helen, keep it Bob on.

Nelly, Pippa and, of course, Mr C… love you.

Introduction

I never deal in scandal, Madam, but one may make use of it as an antidote to itself.[1]

For years, readers have thrilled to the scandalous comings and goings of Julia Quinn's *Bridgerton* novels. Now the books have found a whole new audience with Netflix's smash-hit series, *Bridgerton*, following the ups and downs of the Regency's brightest and most scandalous movers and shakers. Yet for all the stories shared by the mysterious Lady Whistledown, the true tales of Georgian Britain were more than her match. Whilst Lady Whistledown keeps her fictional Regency readers whispering behind their fans about the love lives of their most illustrious contemporaries, the real inhabitants of the United Kingdom had enough gossip to keep them going for years.

Though Lady Whistledown might not be real, in the Georgian era there were still plenty of places to find scandal. People gathered in coffeehouses to pick up the latest gossip and to browse publications including *Town and Country Magazine,* with its must-read *Tête-à-Tête* section. This was one of the earliest forerunners of the modern gossip column and featured a different infamous couple each month. Though no names were mentioned, small silhouettes of the ladies and gents concerned were included alongside each article, accompanied by a breakneck precis of their love lives and most eyebrow-raising escapades. Sharing these salacious tales and trying to identify exactly who each featured couple might be was a common and popular pastime in the era, just as super-injunctions light up social media today. After all, everyone needed to be in the know!

---

1. Walpole, Horace (1844). *Letters of Horace Walpole, Earl of Orford, to Sir Horace Mann, Vol II.* Philadelphia: Lea & Blanchard, p.414.

Lady Whistledown had a forerunner in the splendidly named Mrs Phoebe Crackenthorpe, who was rather archly billed as 'a Lady that knows everything'. Mrs Crackenthorpe was the anonymous author behind *The Female Tatler*, which was published for less than a year between 1709 and 1710. Despite the best efforts of historians, Mrs Crackenthorpe's real identity remains unknown today. The popular magazine is remembered as a gem of early satire despite its brief run, and is all the more remarkable for the fact that it was intended for women. Though its primary aim was to educate – often through sharp social observation and commentary – it had a very well-developed eye for gossip too.

The Female Tatler was the feminine answer to *The Tatler*, which was established by Richard Steele and ran for two years. Under the nom de plume Isaac Bickerstaff, Esquire, Steele published *The Tatler* thrice weekly and shared society news and gossip alongside literary and antiquarian musings. *The Tatler* and *The Female Tatler* were short-lived, but other magazines flourished throughout the eighteenth century and today, our appetite for scandal remains undimmed.

By the dawn of the nineteenth century, though coffeehouse culture was in its death throes and columns such as *Tête-à-Tête* were a thing of the past, the public's need to know was more voracious than ever. It was partly fuelled by a royal family who seemed to be authors of, and magnets for, all manner of eyebrow and petticoat-raising stories. George III was in the care of his doctors, whilst the Prince of Wales had a list of lovers as long as anyone's arm, not to mention one secret wife and one official royal bride from whom he was separated. His brothers were little better and even his isolated sisters managed to get into trouble, much of it unreported.[2] It seemed as though everyone who was anyone was indulging in the sort of behaviour that would make the respectable Lady Bridgerton's hair curl.

Perhaps surprisingly, the Regency era didn't offer whole newspapers dedicated to gossip. The infamous *scandal sheets* emerged in the

---

2. Happily, it is unreported no longer. I tell the stories of the six daughters of George III in my book, *The Daughters of George III: Sisters & Princesses* (Pen & Sword, 2020).

Victorian era and later, but there were still plenty of published rumours to satisfy the public's hunger for thrills. Though the names were usually redacted, the codes used to disguise the identities of their subjects were intentionally easy to see through. Readers were adept at decoding the simple subterfuge and could easily deduce the identity of the Duke of Cumberland from references to *the D— of C—*, whilst an actress might well be referred to as her most celebrated role, rather than her real name. Perhaps the most famous example of these codes came about with the romance of Mary Robinson and the Prince of Wales. The couple began their affair whilst Robinson was playing Perdita in *A Winter's Tale*, and they addressed love notes to one another by the pet names Perdita and Florizel, which was how they were referred to in the press too. Whenever the name of Perdita or Florizel was mentioned, there was no doubt as to whom it referred.

Though gossip kept the wheels of Georgian society turning, not all stories were published with the intention of titillation. Some newspaper proprietors hoped to raise public awareness of corruption, mismanagement or bad behaviour amongst those who ought to know better. James Leigh Hunt famously blew the lid off the Prince Regent's ruinous gambling and spending in *The Examiner* and received a prison sentence for doing so. Theodore Hook, meanwhile, anonymously filled the pages of his weekly magazine, *John Bull*, with gossip about Caroline of Brunswick, the estranged wife of the Prince Regent. Hook was an early forebear of the more notorious type of tabloid journalist that rose to prominence during the twentieth century, hiding his identity and teasing out information by getting to know the servants of the powerful, or simply paying them to disclose sometimes devastating secrets. He was also incredibly well connected and, since his position at the helm of *John Bull* was a secret, Hook was able to gather intelligence organically via the chattering classes in which he moved. Theodore Hook was a trusted confidante of many of his targets and had no qualms about publishing the secrets he promised to keep.

When it came to more generic and perhaps less explosive romantic gossip, readers could follow the comings and goings of the upper classes in the popular *Fashionable World* columns, which were often more concerned with clothes, jewels and the general round of court balls and society events than what happened behind the bedcurtains. Now and then, however, there was a whiff of something a little more clandestine if one was looking out for it.

Scandal reports weren't limited to the written word either. Print shops and printmakers flourished in the Georgian era. Caricatures of the rich and famous were merciless and they skewered scandals and spread gossip just as ably as any newspaper column – often saying far more in pictures than words could convey. For those who couldn't afford to purchase a print, there was always the display in the print shop window where the public could enjoy the most shocking and often lewd examples of the caricaturist's art, without parting with any money. It was a quick and easy way to keep one's finger on the pulse, much like social media trends or the ever-popular celebrity scandal sections of tabloid websites. The likes of Thomas Rowlandson created grotesque and often hilarious – sometimes savagely so – lampoons of celebrities, politicians and royals, exaggerating their shortcomings and hanging out their dirty laundry for the voracious public to devour.

This is a romp through more than a century of scandal, told through twenty-five tales that all have one thing in common: though they might sometimes seem stranger than fiction, they are entirely true. In addition to longer studies, you'll find the occasional *Whisper of Scandal* too: bite-sized chunks of fuel for the fires of the coffeehouse gossips. So, any budding Lady Whistledowns should take note: from the Houses of Parliament to the slums of London, in a century rich with intrigue, there are stories to be told everywhere.

Timeline

The Regency era began in 1811 when King George III, by then foaming at the mouth, blind and mostly immobile, surrendered the throne to his eldest son, George, Prince of Wales. He was to reign initially as Prince Regent and, when his father died nearly a decade later, as King George IV.

The Prince Regent has become a legend amongst British monarchs. A gambler, spendthrift and libertine, he ushered in an age of elegance where fashion, architecture and art found full expression. As the country battled with Napoleon and immense political upheaval, Prinny indulged his every whim, as ostentatious as he was weighty.

It was a time of enormous social contrasts, where opulent fashion and extravagant entertainment glittered, and the great cities of the nation turned their faces towards a new industrialised future. Now a single machine could do the work of a dozen humans, and technology was improving at a breathless pace. Riots and unrest broke out across the country as the populace grew hungry whilst the Regent grew fatter. Regency Britain wasn't only a place of glitter and glitz, but one where life could be miserable. For the Regent at the top of the mountain, those people dwelling in the foothills of poverty barely existed at all.

The Regency saw a country poised on the edge of the modern era, caught between the Age of Enlightenment and the Industrial Revolution. The traditional court of George III, which had clung to a stuffy reliance on piety and protocol, found itself shoved aside by the glittering brilliance of the Prince Regent's gilded life. In the court of the Regent, money talked louder than any language.

During the Regency, it seemed as though England became the hub of the entire world. The streets of London were never quiet, with carriages clattering back and forth every hour of the day and night whilst the government was run not only from Westminster, but from the luxurious confines of Brooks's and White's. In those bastions of the establishment, gentlemen of influence played games not only of cards, but also with the very nation itself.

The Regency was the crowning glory for the kings who had come from Hanover just a century or so earlier. From George I to George IV and beyond, in 100 years, the nation changed forever. This book covers decades of immense change, and this timeline identifies just a few of them.

1714	Reign of George I begins.
1718	First British convicts transported to penal colonies overseas.
1720	The South Sea Bubble bursts.
1721	Robert Walpole becomes de facto first prime minister of Great Britain.
1722	Daniel Defoe's *Moll Flanders* is published.
1727	George I dies; reign of George II begins.
1728	*The Beggar's Opera* premieres in London.
1729	Queen Caroline becomes the first Regent of Great Britain under the Regency Acts when her husband, George II, is out of the country.
1729	Catherine the Great born.
1733	10 Downing Street is occupied by the incumbent prime minister for the first time.
1737	HMS *Victory* is launched.
1738	George III born.
1739	The War of Jenkins's Ear sees Britain declare war on Spain.
1739	Dick Turpin hanged.
1740	The Irish Famine.
1742	Robert Walpole resigns.
1743	George II becomes the last British monarch to lead his army into battle.
1745	Bonnie Prince Charlie lands in Scotland.
1746	The Battle of Culloden.
1751	Parliament passes the Calendar Act, correcting an 11-day discrepancy.

1755	Samuel Johnson's *A Dictionary of the English Language* is published.
1756	Seven Years' War begins.
1759	The British Museum is founded.
1760	George II dies; reign of George III begins.
1761	George III and Charlotte of Mecklenburg-Strelitz marry.
1762	George IV (also known as the Prince Regent) born.
1763	Seven Years' War ends.
1770	Louis XVI and Marie Antoinette marry.
1770	Captain James Cook lands at Botany Bay.
1771	Britain's first cotton mill opens.
1773	The Boston Tea Party.
1775	American War of Independence begins.
1775	Jane Austen born.
1776	U.S. Declaration of Independence signed.
1783	American War of Independence ends.
1785	George IV and Maria Fitzherbert marry.
1786	Frederick the Great dies.
1788	George III's mental illness brings about the Regency Crisis.
1788	Lord Byron born.
1789	The Bastille falls.
1789	The French Revolution begins.
1789	George Washington becomes first U.S. president.
1791	William Wilberforce's bill to abolish slavery is rejected.
1791	Thomas Boswell's *Life of Johnson* is published.
1792	Mary Wollstonecraft's *A Vindication of the Rights of Women* is published.
1793	The Reign of Terror.
1793	Louis XVI and Marie Antoinette executed.
1795	George IV and Caroline of Brunswick marry.
1796	Edward Jenner introduces vaccination against smallpox.
1796	Catherine the Great dies.
1796	Princess Charlotte of Wales, heir to the throne and the only child of George IV and Caroline of Brunswick, is born.
1799	The French Revolution ends.

1799	Income Tax is introduced in Great Britain.
1800	George III survives two assassination attempts.
1800	The Acts of Union unite the Kingdom of Great Britain and the Kingdom of Ireland into one United Kingdom.
1802	Marie Tussaud opens her first waxwork exhibit in the United Kingdom.
1803	The Napoleonic Wars begin.
1804	Napoleon proclaimed Emperor of the French.
1805	The Royal Navy triumphs at Trafalgar, though Admiral Nelson is killed.
1806	William Pitt the Younger dies.
1806	The Holy Roman Empire falls.
1807	*An Act for the Abolition of the Slave Trade* is passed in the House of Commons.
1808	The slave trade is abolished in the British colonies.
1809	Daniel Lambert, the fattest man in Britain, dies.
1810	Lord Byron swims across the Hellespont in Turkey.
1810	George III is declared insane.
1811	The Prince of Wales becomes the Prince Regent; the Regency begins.
1811	The Luddite movement begins.
1812	Prime Minister Spencer Perceval is assassinated.
1813	Fourteen Luddites are hanged at York.
1814	The First Bourbon Restoration.
1815	The Hundred Days.
1815	Napoleon is defeated by Wellington at Waterloo; the Napoleonic Wars end.
1815	The Congress of Vienna concludes.
1815	The Second Bourbon Restoration.
1816	The year without a summer.
1817	Jane Austen dies.
1817	The first cholera pandemic begins.
1817	Princess Charlotte of Wales dies.
1818	Charlotte of Mecklenburg-Strelitz dies.
1819	The Peterloo Massacre.

1820	George III dies; reign of George IV begins.
1820	The Pains and Penalties Bill puts Queen Caroline on trial.
1820	The Cato Street Conspiracy to murder the Cabinet is foiled.
1821	Napoleon dies.
1821	Elizabeth Fry establishes the British Ladies' Society for Promoting the Reformation of Female Prisoners.
1821	Caroline of Brunswick dies.
1822	Percy Bysshe Shelley dies.
1823	Mary Anning finds the first complete Plesiosaurus skeleton.
1824	Lord Byron dies.
1825	The Stockton and Darlington Railway, the world's first modern railway, opens.
1826	The United Kingdom experiences the second hottest summer on record.
1826	The second cholera pandemic begins.
1827	The Duke of Wellington becomes Commander-in-Chief of the Forces.
1827	The Duke of Wellington becomes prime minister.
1828	The trial of Burke and Hare begins.
1829	The Metropolitan Police Service is established.
1830	George IV dies; reign of William IV begins.
1831	Charles Darwin embarks on his voyage aboard HMS *Beagle*.
1832	The second cholera pandemic reaches London.
1833	The Slavery Abolition Act receives Royal Assent.
1833	The Factory Act makes it illegal to employ children under the age of 9 in factories.
1833	Abolitionist William Wilberforce dies.
1834	The Tolpuddle Martyrs are sentenced to transportation.
1834	Fire sweeps through the Palace of Westminster.
1834	William IV dismisses the government and appoints Wellington as prime minister; this is the last time a British monarch appoints a prime minister against the will of Parliament.
1835	Madame Tussauds opens in Baker Street.
1836	Charles Darwin concludes his voyage on HMS *Beagle*.
1837	William IV dies.
1837	Reign of Queen Victoria begins.

A Regency Glossary

Though the Georgian era is not a difficult one in which to immerse oneself, occasionally the specific terms of the period can seem like a different language. This basic glossary of the period should help budding Bridgertonians find their feet!

Abigail	A lady's maid.
Accouchement	Labour and the 'lying-in' period prior to it.
Affair of honour	A duel.
Ague	A feverish complaint.
Almack's	Exclusive assembly rooms on King Street, London. Admission was strictly controlled by the lady patronesses, at a cost of 10 guineas per year.
Almshouses	Charity homes for the poor and elderly.
Apoplexy	A stroke.
Apothecary	A herbal practitioner.
Assembly rooms	Place where dances and social events were held.
Assizes	Courts outside London, which met twice-yearly.
Banns	Public announcement of the intention to marry, read in church for three weeks prior to the wedding.
Bedlam	The Hospital of Saint Mary of Bethlehem, an asylum in London.
Bluestocking	An intellectual woman.
Bluestocking Society	A place where women could meet to discuss intellectual matters.
Bourdaloue	The answer to the question: 'how did they pee in those dresses?'.

Bow Street Runner	The forerunners of the Metropolitan Police.
Brooks's	A celebrated gentleman's club in Regency London; favoured by Whigs.
Chit	A flighty girl.
Cit	Derogatory term for a merchant.
Coffeehouse	A place to drink coffee, debate and set the world to rights.
Coming out	A young lady's debut in society, and the start of her search for a husband.
Consumption	Tuberculosis.
Corinthian	A man of fashion.
Courtesan	A high-class sex worker.
Court of Arches	The highest ecclesiastical court, in which crim con cases were often heard.
Court of St James's	The official home of the British royal court.
Crim con	Criminal Conversation. A legal measure by which a husband may sue any man who has sex with his wife, unless the married couple is already separated.
Cut	To publicly snub someone. To give someone *the cut direct* was a public snub to their face, whilst *the cut indirect* meant simply to pretend not to notice them. The *cut sublime* involved admiring something high off the ground such as a building or even the clouds, until the coast was clear. Finally, *the cut infernal* was given by looking at the ground until the snubbed person had passed.
Cyprian	Another high-class sex worker.
Dandy	A fashionable fellow.
Debutante	A young lady who has just 'come out'.
Demi-monde	Those on the glamorous fringes of society, such as courtesans, sex workers or theatricals.
Divorce	Exactly what it means today. However, women could not petition for divorce, and it had to be

	granted by an Act of Parliament. This meant that it was outside the reach of all but the wealthy.
Doctors' Commons	The rooms where those practising civil law could be found.
Dowager	The widow of a titled man; the term is assumed after the heir marries.
Doxy	A sex worker.
Entail	Inherited property which cannot be sold, but passes through the line of inheritance via direct heirs.
Fashionable hour	Specifically 4.30pm-7.30pm in London, when the ton promenaded or rode in Hyde Park.
Fleet Prison	Debtors' prison.
Gentleman	A man whose family had sufficient assets to allow him to live comfortably without working.
Guinea	A gold coin worth 21 shillings.
Hell	A gambling den.
Hoyden	A boisterous girl.
Jointure	A widow's financial provision.
La Belle Assemblée	A Regency magazine focusing on upper-class fashions.
Macaroni	A flamboyant fellow.
Masque	A costume ball.
Modiste	A dressmaker.
Nabob	An English gentleman who made his fortune in India.
Newgate	London's most infamous prison.
Old Bailey	Central London courts.
On dit	Gossip.
Pink of the ton	A chap who is the height of male fashion.
Pleasure gardens	A place of bucolic entertainment in which the fashionable liked to be seen.
Prince Regent	George, Prince of Wales, became Prince Regent in 1811 with the indisposition of his

	father, King George III. He reigned as Regent until he assumed the throne as George IV in 1820.
Prison hulk	Ships on which convicts were held.
Quack	An unqualified or charlatan doctor.
Queen Charlotte's Ball	An annual royal ball at which debutantes were presented to the queen and hoped to find an eligible bachelor.
Rake	A scoundrel.
The Regency	The period 1811–1820, under the reign of the Prince Regent.
Rotten Row	A fashionable path on which to ride in Hyde Park.
Season	The social season, which began in spring and ended when Parliament returned.
Snuff	Powdered tobacco; Queen Charlotte's biggest vice.
Special licence	A sought-after and expensive marriage licence from the Archbishop of Canterbury, allowing marriage at any time or place.
Taking the waters	The act of visiting a spa town to bathe or drink the mineral waters found there for one's health.
Ton	Fashionable society.
Town	London, the centre of the Regency universe.
Vauxhall Gardens	A pleasure garden in which to be seen.
White's	The oldest and most celebrated gentleman's club in Regency London; favoured by Tories.

The Social Classes

Social class was the driving force of Georgian Britain. It could dictate everything from one's opportunities to one's life expectancy and observing their so-called *proper place* was a skill every person was expected to learn. Though terms such as upper, middle, and working class are easy enough to interpret, in his 1814 book, *Treatise on the Wealth, Power and Resources of the British Empire*, Patrick Colquhoun breaks down the class distinction even further into the following categories. It is an interesting insight into the complications of class and money during the Regency.

Highest Orders | The Royal Family, the Lords Spiritual and Temporal, the Great Officers of State, and all above the degree of a Baronet, with their families.

Second Class | Baronets, Knights, Country Gentlemen, and others having large incomes, with their families.

Third Class | Dignified Clergy, Persons holding considerable employments in the State, elevated situations in the Law, eminent Practitioners in Physic, considerable Merchants, Manufacturers upon a large scale, and Bankers of the first order, with their families.

Fourth Class | Persons holding inferior situations in Church and State, respectable Clergymen of different persuasions, Practitioners in Law and Physic, Teachers of Youth of the superior order, respectable Freeholders, Ship Owners, Merchants and Manufacturers of the second class, Warehousemen and respectable Shopkeepers, Artists, respectable Builders, Mechanics, and Persons living on moderate incomes, with their families.

Fifth Class	Lower Freeholders, Shopkeepers of the second order, Innkeepers, Publicans, and Persons engaged in miscellaneous occupations of living on moderate incomes, with their families.
Sixth Class	Working Mechanics, Artisans, Handicrafts, Agricultural Labourers, and others who subsist by labour in various employments with their families. Menial servants.
Seventh Class	Paupers and their families, Vagrants, Gipsies, Rogues, Vagabonds, and idle and disorderly persons, supported by criminal delinquency.
Army and Navy	Officers of the Army, Navy, and Marines, including all Officers on half-pay and superannuated, with their families.
	Non-commissioned Officers in the Army, Navy, and Marines, Soldiers, Seamen, and Marines, including Pensioners of the Army, Navy, &c. and their families.

Cast of Characters

The scandalous stars of these stories are many and their families are often intertwined. To make navigating the gossipy waters easier, here's the rundown of our leading players.

Elizabeth Armistead	Celebrated courtesan and philanthropist. Wife of Charles James Fox.
Mary Beauclerk	Daughter of Topham Beauclerk and Lady Diana Spencer. Lover of her own half-brother, George, 3rd Viscount Bolingbroke.
Topham Beauclerk	Lover and later husband of Lady Diana Spencer. Father of Mary Beauclerk.
William Beckford	The Fool of Fonthill. Builder of tall towers and lover of William Courtenay, 9th Earl of Devon.
Mariana Belcombe	Lover of Anne Lister.
Joseph Biscoe	Husband of Susanna Hope and best friend of her lover, Robert Home Gordon.
Charles Blessington	1st Earl of Blessington. Husband of Marguerite, Countess of Blessington.
Marguerite Blessington	Countess of Blessington. Wife of Charles, 1st Earl of Blessington, and rumoured lover of Alfred, Count d'Orsay.
Caroline of Brunswick	Wife of George IV, uncrowned queen and keen on fun. Lover of Bartolomeo Pergami.
Eleanor Butler	Partner of Sarah Ponsonby, lady of Llangollen.
George Byron	6th Baron Byron. Yes, *that* one. Lover of Lady Caroline Lamb. Mad, bad and dangerous to know.

Elizabeth Chudleigh	Duchess of Kingston. Wife of Evelyn Pierrepont, 2nd Duke of Kingston-upon-Hull. Also wife of Augustus Hervey, 3rd Earl of Bristol. The Duchess-Countess.
William Courtenay	9th Earl of Devon. Lover of William Beckford.
Lavinia Fenton	Duchess of Bolton. Opera star, lover and later wife of Charles Powlett, 3rd Duke of Bolton.
Kitty Fisher	Courtesan and megastar. Lover of George Coventry, 6th Earl of Coventry, and sworn enemy of Maria, Countess of Coventry.
Maria Fitzherbert	Secret wife of George IV. Long-suffering.
John FitzPatrick	2nd Earl of Upper Ossory. Lover and later husband of Anne Liddell.
Augustus Henry FitzRoy	3rd Duke of Grafton. Prime minister. Husband of Anne Liddell. Lover of Anne Parsons.
Charles James Fox	Leader of the Opposition. Husband of Elizabeth Armistead.
George IV	King, Prince Regent, Prince of Wales and all-round bad egg. Son of George III and Queen Charlotte. Husband of Maria Fitzherbert and Caroline of Brunswick. Lover of too many to mention.
Robert Home Gordon	Lover of Susanna Hope and best friend of her husband, Joseph Biscoe.
Henrietta Grosvenor	Countess Grosvenor. Wife of Richard, 1st Earl Grosvenor, and lover of Prince Henry, Duke of Cumberland and Strathearn.
Richard Grosvenor	1st Earl Grosvenor. Husband of Henrietta, Countess Grosvenor.
Elizabeth Gunning	1st Baroness Hamilton of Hameldon. Wife of James Hamilton, 6th Duke of Hamilton. Mother of Elizabeth Smith-Stanley, Countess of Derby.
Maria Gunning	Countess of Coventry. Wife of George Coventry, 6th Earl of Coventry, lover of

	Frederick St John, 2nd Viscount Bolingbroke. Sworn enemy of Kitty Fisher.
James Hackman	Murderer of Martha Ray.
Emma Hamilton	*The* Lady Hamilton. Wife of William Hamilton, lover of Nelson. Mother of Horatia Nelson.
James Hamilton	6th Duke of Hamilton. Husband of Elizabeth Gunning. Father of Elizabeth Smith-Stanley, Countess of Derby.
William Hamilton	Husband of Lady Emma.
Prince Henry	Duke of Cumberland and Strathearn. Brother of George III and lover of Henrietta, Countess Grosvenor.
Elizabeth Herbert	Countess of Pembroke. Wife of Henry Herbert, 10th Earl of Pembroke. Sister of Lady Diana Spencer.
Henry Herbert	10th Earl of Pembroke. Husband of Elizabeth Herbert. Lover of Kitty Hunter.
Augustus Hervey	3rd Earl of Bristol. Husband of Elizabeth Chudleigh.
Susanna Hope	Wife of Joseph Biscoe and lover of his best friend, Robert Home Gordon.
Kitty Hunter	Lover of Henry Herbert, 10th Earl of Pembroke.
Percy Jocelyn	Bishop of Clogher. Would-be lover of James Moverley.
Caroline Lamb	Wife of William, 2nd Viscount Melbourne, and lover of Lord Byron.
William Lamb	2nd Viscount Melbourne. Prime minister and husband of Lady Caroline Lamb. Did not make eyes at a young Queen Victoria.
Anne Liddell	Duchess of Grafton. Wife of Augustus FitzRoy, 3rd Duke of Grafton. Lover and later wife of John FitzPatrick, 2nd Earl of Upper Ossory.

Anne Lister	AKA Gentleman Jack, the lady of Shibden Hall. Lover of Mariana Belcombe. Wife of Ann Walker.
Henry St John Mildmay	4th Baronet. Lover of Harriet, Countess of Rosebery.
John Montagu	4th Earl of Sandwich. Lover of Martha Ray.
James Moverley	Would-be lover of Percy Jocelyn, Bishop of Clogher.
Frances Nelson	Viscountess Nelson. Wife of *the* Nelson.
Horatia Nelson	Daughter of Lady Hamilton and Lord Nelson.
Horatio Nelson	1st Viscount Nelson. Husband of Frances, Viscountess Nelson. Lover of Emma Hamilton and father of Horatia Nelson.
Alfred d'Orsay	Count d'Orsay. Rumoured lover of Charles and Marguerite, Earl and Countess of Blessington.
Anne Parsons	Known as Nancy. Courtesan and lover of Augustus FitzRoy, 3rd Duke of Grafton.
Bartolomeo Pergami	Lover of Caroline of Brunswick.
Evelyn Pierrepont	2nd Duke of Kingston-upon-Hull. Husband of Elizabeth Chudleigh.
Sarah Ponsonby	Partner of Lady Eleanor Butler, lady of Llangollen.
Charles Powlett	3rd Duke of Bolton. Married Lavinia Fenton.
Archibald Primrose	4th Earl of Rosebery. Husband of Harriet, Countess of Rosebery.
Harriet Primrose	Countess of Rosebery. Wife of Archibald, 4th Earl of Rosebery. Lover of Sir Henry St John-Mildmay.
Martha Ray	Lover of John Montagu, 4th Earl of Sandwich. Murdered by James Hackman.
John Sackville	3rd Duke of Dorset. Lover of Anne Parsons and Elizabeth Smith-Stanley, Countess of Derby
Frances Scudamore	Duchess of Beaufort. Lover of William, 2nd Baron Talbot.

Edward Smith-Stanley	12th Earl of Derby. Husband of Elizabeth Smith-Stanley, Countess of Derby.
Elizabeth Smith-Stanley	Countess of Derby. Daughter of Elizabeth, Baroness Hamilton of Hameldon, and James, 6th Duke of Hamilton. Wife of Edward Smith-Stanley, 12th Earl of Derby. Lover of John Sackville, 3rd Duke of Dorset.
Henry Somerset	3rd Duke of Beaufort. Husband of Frances Scudamore.
Diana Spencer	Viscountess Bolingbroke. Wife of Frederick St John, 2nd Viscount Bolingbroke. Lover and later wife of Topham Beauclerk. Mother of George, 3rd Viscount Bolingbroke, and Mary Beauclerk.
Charlotte St John	Viscountess Bolingbroke. Wife of George, 3rd Viscount Bolingbroke.
Frederick St John	2nd Viscount Bolingbroke. AKA Bully the Battersea Baron. Husband of Lady Diana Spencer. Father of George, 3rd Viscount Bolingbroke. Lover of Maria Gunning.
George St John	3rd Viscount Bolingbroke. Son of Frederick, 2nd Viscount Bolingbroke, and Lady Diana Spencer. Husband of Charlotte, Viscountess Bolingbroke. Lover of his own half-sister, Mary Beauclerk.
William Talbot	2nd Baron Talbot. Lover of Frances Scudamore, Duchess of Beaufort.
Catherine Tylney-Long	Richest commoner in England. Wife of William Wellesley-Pole.
Ann Walker	Wife of Anne Lister.
William Wellesley-Pole	All-round bad egg. Husband of Catherine Tylney-Long.
Harriette Wilson	Canny courtesan and author. Lover of many illustrious men.

Duchess Polly and the Duke of Bolton

In which Polly Peachum captures the heart of a duke…

Bath, July the 6th, 1728.

The d— of —, I hear, hath run away with *Polly Peachum*, having settled 400*l.* a Year upon her during Pleasure; and upon Disagreement, 200*l.* a Year![1]

On 29 January 1728, John Gay's *The Beggar's Opera* premiered at the Lincoln's Inn Fields Theatre in London. The show was a smash hit and catapulted one of its leads to overnight superstardom. As the curtain fell, the name on everyone's lips was that of 19-year-old Lavinia Fenton, who had been plucked from obscurity and handed the plum role of Polly Peachum. It was to make her name and her fortune.

At first glance Lavinia seemed to be the perfect casting for Polly: a pretty innocent whose naïve façade hides a smart, impassioned nature. Indeed, *The Beggar's Opera* might almost have seemed like a study of the life she had once known, for she was no privileged young lady. Just as Gay's satirical work laid bare the mean streets of London to show an underbelly populated by characters who were both exploited by, and exploiting, their so-called betters, Lavinia had experienced life at the sharp end. By the time Charles Powlett, the 42-year-old 3rd Duke of Bolton, began his nightly visits to the theatre, Lavinia Fenton was already the toast of the town.

Like so many of her contemporaries, Lavinia's early life is shrouded in mystery, her exact origins lost in a haze of half-truths and PR. When

---

1. Hawkesworth, John (ed.) (1766). *Letters, Written by the Late Jonathan Swift, DD.* London: T. Davies, p.94.

her father, a man named Beswick, abandoned her pregnant mother and returned to the Royal Navy, never to be seen again, the enterprising woman married a coffeehouse keeper named Fenton and set up business in Charing Cross. There, young Lavinia entertained the patrons with songs and witty stories, whilst her mother was busy negotiating a new domestic and business arrangement for her adolescent daughter. Under this agreement Lavinia would become the kept lover of a mysterious man known only as the Feathered Gull, and receive £200 a year for her services. But Lavinia wasn't willing to be sold to a man she hadn't chosen and struck out alone. By the time she was in her mid-teens, she was earning her keep as a courtesan.

Yet Lavinia wasn't destined to become a career courtesan in the style of Kitty Fisher or Mrs Armistead. She can little have guessed how high she would climb, but she was determined to make her own way in the world. In 1726 one of the coffeehouse's patrons offered Lavinia a role in Thomas Otway's *The Orphan*. For the young woman who had already made such a splash by entertaining visitors to the coffeehouse, this was a natural career progression and Lavinia grabbed it with both hands.

Lavinia's good looks and charm made her a natural on stage, and she was soon climbing the bill as a member of the company at Lincoln's Inn Fields Theatre. It was there, in 1728, that she eventually landed the plum role of Polly Peachum for the premiere performance of *The Beggar's Opera*. She was such a hit that people began to refer to her by the name of her character, and a steady stream of admirers trod a path to the stage door, hoping to woo Polly Peachum. Prints of Lavinia in character became big sellers, and balladeers sang songs in praise of her beauty. One of those who fell under her spell was the Duke of Bolton, and soon the theatre at Lincoln's Inn Fields was his nightly destination.

Charles Powlett had enjoyed a long, if not particularly distinguished, career as a Whig politician before he inherited his father's dukedom and was elevated to the House of Lords. More than twenty years Lavinia's senior, the former wayward youth had become a pillar of the establishment, and Lord Bolton was now a Privy Councillor who had served as Lord Justice. He was also married, and had been since 1713. The Duchess of Bolton was Lady Anne Vaughan, daughter of the 3rd

Earl of Carbery, and the Boltons' childless union was anything but happy. It was a marriage that had been forced on Powlett by his father, who had once been dismissed by Jonathan Swift as 'a great booby'. Soon after the death of the 2nd Duke in 1722, Charles and Lady Anne became permanently estranged; all the duchess asked for was a £1,000 annuity, and she was given it without complaint.

It was a footloose and fancy-free Duke of Bolton who gadded along to the theatre each evening to gaze at Polly Peachum, and his presence didn't go unnoticed for long. When William Hogarth painted a scene from the opera featuring Lavinia, he made sure to include her besotted would-be beau, making doe eyes at her from his box at the side of the stage. Yet it wasn't only Hogarth who was intrigued by the duke's fascination with Lavinia. Lady Anne was just as keen as everyone else to get a look at the celebrated Miss Fenton, and the Duke of Bolton was shocked to find his wife in his box one evening waiting for the curtain to rise.

Becoming mistress to a titled or rich man in the Georgian era was as much a matter of business as of the heart, and the Duke of Bolton knew precisely what was required of him if he was to secure Lavinia's favours ahead of his many rivals. He offered her a deal, promising to pay her £400 a year for as long as they were together, and £200 a year if their relationship didn't work out. On top of that, she would receive a fine house in Mayfair and every luxury that his money could buy.

Of course, Lavinia said yes. She retired at the tender age of 20 after more than sixty performances as Polly Peachum, and became mistress to the Duke of Bolton. Given that Lord Bolton had spent his lifetime in the pursuit of pleasure, nobody expected the relationship to be anything other than a passing fancy. They were sure that Lavinia would soon be back on the casting rounds, and the Duke of Bolton would be sampling the delights of London once more. Yet in that house in Mayfair, Lavinia and Lord Bolton found that they had everything they could possibly want. They settled down to a life of domesticity, albeit one between man and mistress, not husband and wife.

Though Lord Bolton made no effort to seek a divorce, in every other respect he and Lavinia lived as though they were married. In Georgian

England, the sanctity of wedding vows was rather elastic when it came to the rich and, just like today, money talked. Lavinia became her lover's acknowledged companion, acting as his hostess at his Greenwich home, Westcombe House, and was seen on his arm at all the best parties. Lavinia bore the duke three sons[2] and the little family lived in harmony within Westcombe's palatial walls. Lavinia and the Duke of Bolton remained a happy and faithful couple for more than twenty years.

By 1751 Lady Anne's health was frail and her death was expected to come sooner, rather than later. Keen to escape the renewed interest in their relationship that they knew Lady Anne's death would bring about, the duke and Lavinia hastened to France. They were accompanied by chaplain Joseph Warton, who married the couple as soon as news came of the Duchess of Bolton's passing. With that wedding, the coffeehouse courtesan became the brand-new Duchess of Bolton. Yet Lavinia's married life was short and just three years after their wedding, the duke died. The heartbroken duchess outlived her beloved husband by just six years. She died aged 52 in January 1760.

There is a curious, extremely Georgian postscript to the tale of Lavinia Fenton, and one that perfectly illustrates the twists and turns of fate in this most scandalous time. When Lavinia retired from her celebrated role as Polly Peachum, the part was taken by Maria Warren, who never scaled the dizzying heights of her predecessor. In fact, whilst Lavinia ended up in a mansion, Maria found herself in Newgate, charged with bigamy.

At first, Maria's solicitor tried for an impressive sleight of hand, pointing out that the Act of Parliament that forbade bigamy mentioned only that a man could not have more than one wife. The law made no mention of a woman taking more than one husband. Therefore, he argued, Maria could not have been said to have broken *any* law. The gambit failed and after some back and forth about the exact nature and extent of the Act as written and intended, the trial proceeded. Luckily for Maria, the witnesses for the prosecution were anything but clear

---

2. Since the couple's sons were illegitimate, none could inherit the dukedom. Instead, they went on to have careers in the military and the church.

on exactly what had transpired, and she was acquitted. Mrs Warren, the lesser Polly Peachum, was a free woman once more, if not quite a duchess.

A Whisper of Scandal: A Fancy for a Footman

Susan Montagu, Duchess of Manchester, was the mother of eight children by her notoriously unfaithful husband, who left her at home alone whilst he served as Governor of Jamaica. In reply, she gave him up for a footman, and was ostracised from polite society for the rest of her days.

Witness to the Masturbation

In which a peer must prove his potency…

> The privy members of the Duke were never to my knowledge turgid, dilated or erected in such a way as (in my opinion) may be usual and necessary to perform the act of carnal copulation.[1]

Henry Somerset, 3rd Duke of Beaufort, was born to privilege. By the age of 7, he had inherited one of the most valuable dukedoms in the land and held the keys to the magnificent Badminton House. His life seemed to be charmed, and when he married the enormously wealthy Frances, only child of James Scudamore, 3rd Viscount Scudamore, in 1729, it seemed as though the match was made in heaven. Or rather, financial heaven at least. This was not a love match, but one of business and money, and Henry even changed his name to Scudamore to cement his claim to his bride's enormous wealth.

Despite its beginnings, the marriage was happy, if not blissful, but as the years passed and no heir was born, the couple drifted apart. When Lady Frances met William, 2nd Baron Talbot[2], in 1740, sparks inevitably flew. As a Whig politician, the married Lord Talbot was the natural political opponent of the Tory Duke of Beaufort, but they were to go head-to-head on matters far more personal than politics.

The Talbots and the Beauforts had a few important things in common that paved the way for scandal. Talbot's marriage, like that of the Beauforts, had been for money, and his wife's health was poor, as

---

1. McLaren, Angus (2007). *Impotence: A Cultural History*. Chicago: University of Chicago Press, p.72.
2. Later Earl Talbot.

was that of Lord Beaufort. Whilst Lady Talbot languished at home, her husband and Lady Frances embarked on a passionate affair. Their secret meetings were held at Lady Beaufort's home in Grosvenor Square, but they weren't quite as clandestine as the lovers hoped. When a servant stumbled upon Lady Frances perched in the half-naked Lord Talbot's lap, the jig was up. He hurried to the servants' hall and told his colleagues exactly what was going on above stairs. When Talbot visited again several days later and the couple locked the door of the dining room, members of the household listened at the keyhole. They heard the duchess fretting that the servants suspected their tryst before, most incriminating of all, she breathlessly told Talbot, 'You make me so hot.' The secret was a secret no longer, and the couple knew it.

In their efforts to escape discovery, Lord Talbot and Lady Frances resorted to meeting in the countryside. After arriving at the appointed place, Lady Frances would leave her horse with groom John Pember, then climb into Talbot's carriage for a quick rendezvous. As Pember waited behind the enthusiastically rocking vehicle, one wonders just how Lady Frances thought they would escape detection.

Pember, of course, couldn't wait to tell everyone what he had seen, but he offered to hold his tongue... for a price. Lady Beaufort and Lord Talbot paid the groom more than two years' worth of wages to keep his mouth shut, but by then it was too late. Their affair was the talk of the Beaufort household, and it was only a matter of time before Lord Beaufort learned what was afoot.

At first, the duke tried to keep the unseemly matter out of the public eye. A private separation was drawn up in 1740 and the couple parted ways amicably, even enjoying dinner together on the last evening before their marriage effectively ended. For the next two years, however, the Duke of Beaufort fretted. His already fragile health failed and he became ever more restless at reports of his estranged wife's unashamed cavorting with Lord Talbot. Lord Talbot was keen to ensure that his own wife didn't learn of the affair, but when Lady Frances fell pregnant, the game was up. With servants regularly observing their trysts and the price to keep them quiet getting higher by the day, something had to give.

The couple's baby girl was born in secret and smuggled away to London, where she was baptised as Fanny Matthews. Sadly, Fanny didn't live more than a few weeks, but the baby's birth marked the beginning of the end for the Beaufort-Talbot affair. Lady Frances had refused to come to London as her due date approached, preferring the country air to the city fug. Her obstinacy enraged Talbot, as did the sheer amount of cash that he had been doling out to servants, wet nurses and midwives just to keep the pregnancy a secret. By the spring of 1742, the affair was over.

It was then that Lord Beaufort made his move, and Lady Frances was blindsided. He sued his wife's lover for criminal conversation – adultery – in the Court of Arches, the highest ecclesiastical court. He secured statements from the midwife who had delivered the baby, from household servants and even John Pember, who had extorted so much money from his employer and her lover. Faced with the crim con suit and stung by her abandonment and her servants' betrayal, Lady Frances countersued. She hit back with the explosive claim that she had no choice but to take a lover because her husband was impotent. Lord Talbot followed her example and argued that his wife's ill health had left him sexually frustrated. What else could he do but commit adultery?

The trial was London's biggest talking point, and nothing was out of bounds. The court thrilled to descriptions of Lady Beaufort and Lord Talbot making love on chairs, in carriages, in fields and everything in between. The scandalised witnesses described Talbot suckling the milk from Lady Frances' breasts to drain them, and of wild and spontaneous sexual escapades with little thought for concealment. Lady Frances came back swinging. She had never even consummated her marriage, she argued, because her husband was incapable of doing so.

Rumours were rife that the Duke of Beaufort had at least one illegitimate child in the form of Margaret Burr, later the wife of Thomas Gainsborough, but he didn't produce her to refute the charge of impotence. Instead, he agreed to allow a team of physicians to watch him masturbate, which would prove his potency once and for all. 'I should never have been potent again!' joked Horace Walpole as he described the scene in the house of a Dr Meade. As the physicians waited, Beaufort masturbated behind a screen until he called them forward to witness his ejaculation. Suitably satisfied by such undeniable evidence, the doctors concluded that impotency was no defence for the duchess. Her case was thrown out and Beaufort sued Talbot for thousands. Perhaps surprisingly, Lady Frances and Lord Talbot revelled in it. They reunited for a while and rode the wave of infamy, but the cracks soon showed once more.

Though the Court of Arches could, and did, confirm adultery, it did not have the power to grant a divorce. For this, Beaufort needed to present his case to the House of Lords and he did so in the closing days of 1743. As the Lords gathered in January 1744 to review the evidence, there was standing room only; the gentlemen of the Upper House were as keen as anyone to hear the saucy details. They concluded the case within weeks, and the Beaufort divorce was final.

Lord Beaufort died in February 1745, by which time it was all change for his ex-wife and her former lover too. Talbot separated from his wife and never took another, but the duchess wasn't about to be kept down. She married Charles FitzRoy, who also took the Scudamore name, and was the illegitimate son of the Duke of Grafton and half-brother of another of our scandalous leading men. In Georgian Britain, nothing happened in a vacuum.

A Whisper of Scandal: The Brazen Baroness

Catherine Ball, aka the Baroness de Calabrella, left her royal chaplain husband for her lover, Captain George de Blaquiere. When her abandoned husband committed suicide, she took de Blaquiere's name and headed off to a new life in Italy as the grand-sounding Baroness de Calabrella.

The Courtesan and the Countess

In which two celebrated ladies go to war…

> I SING not of wars or invasions,
> I tell you a merrier tale –
> How Fisher and Covey were met, Sir,
> And sent all the people to gaol.
>
> The one was a modest-faced sinner,
> The other a quality toast.
>
> But Covey could not bear a rival;
> She thought it a terrible case
> That first they should gaze at Kate Fisher,
> And then come and stare in her face.

In Georgian Britain, Kitty Fisher was a bona fide megastar. She was famous for simply *being*, and a forerunner of the modern personalities we know today: a star because she was a star. Little is known of her early life, and what information exists is a mixture of fact and romance with plenty of misdirection, no doubt provided by Kitty herself to maintain her mystique. Of the few apparently indisputable facts that exist, one is that she was born to poor parents in 1741 and the second is that, by the age of 17, Kitty was already a celebrated and sought-after courtesan. Like so many other women in Georgian London, she wasn't content to stay poor forever, and sex work was the path she chose to leave her poverty behind.

Admiral Augustus Keppel was credited with being Kitty's first illustrious client, but he was certainly not the last. She gathered patrons and scandal with voracious abandon, and gossips fell over themselves to spread her legend around the town. Casanova found Kitty charming and claimed he saw her eat a 1,000-guinea banknote on a slice of bread and butter. When she fell from her horse in St James's Park in 1759, it was a matter of great press interest that the celebrated Miss Fisher had flashed her unmentionables. And Kitty turned notoriety into cash.

Kitty Fisher was an eighteenth-century influencer, and glamorous young women sought to emulate her fashionable looks and ways. Prints showing her likeness became bestsellers, and pamphlets detailing her escapades and charms were produced by the dozen, whilst Sir Joshua Reynolds made her his muse, capturing her likeness in some of his most celebrated works. People simply couldn't get enough of Miss Kitty Fisher and she knew better than anyone how to play the PR game. Indeed, Kitty even printed and distributed her own pamphlets, which promised not only a night to remember, but a side order of intelligence and a garnish of ready wit too.

The divine Miss Fisher was not the only woman to make something out of very little indeed. The Gunning sisters may have been born into a noble lineage, as granddaughters of the 6th Viscount Mayo, but their family was far from wealthy. When Maria Gunning and her sister Elizabeth came of age, their mother sent them to Ireland to begin careers in the theatre. This was far from a respectable profession for a young lady of breeding, but breeding alone wasn't enough to pay the bills.

Beautiful, intelligent and sparky, the two Gunning sisters soon attracted admiring attention and were welcomed into London high society. Kitty Fisher was still building her client list by the time the Gunning sisters were marrying into money, privilege and rank. Elizabeth made it to the upper tier in scandalous style, attracting the attention of the 6th Duke of Hamilton, whom Horace Walpole memorably described as 'hot, debauched, extravagant, and equally damaged in his fortune and person'. When she and the duke found themselves at a ball at Bedford House on Valentine's Day in 1752, Lord Hamilton could restrain himself no longer. He called for a parson and demanded that he and Elizabeth be married there and then. The parson refused, so the couple leapt into a carriage and were married at Mayfair Chapel that same night, with a humble ring torn from a bed curtain serving to mark the union. They became the parents of a young lady whose notoriety we'll examine elsewhere in this volume. Maria, meanwhile, married the 6th Earl of Coventry in 1752. When the blushing bride said her vows, she had no idea that she was about to get into a very public, very embarrassing spat with none other than the notorious Kitty Fisher.

As the Countess of Coventry, the beautiful and fashionable Maria Gunning flourished. Her celebrity status was cemented when she had to take a bodyguard along while out for a walk, just to keep her adoring fans at bay. Maria revelled in the attention, keeping up appearances even as her marriage began to falter. The earl hated her devotion to cosmetics and forbade her to wear her favourite rouge; when she defied him, he wiped the make-up off in public as though she was a child. Policing his wife's cosmetics didn't take up all of his time though, and eventually the 6th Earl of Coventry found his way to Kitty Fisher's bedroom. There were rumours of Lady Coventry's own extra-marital liaisons with a list of men, including the notorious Lord Bolingbroke (more of him later) that contemporaries feared might lead Lord Coventry to seek a divorce. However, she considered herself to be all the woman a man might need. At the thought of her husband and the courtesan, Maria was not impressed.

The soap opera that Horace Walpole termed the *Gunninghiad* gripped polite society. Lady Coventry's fury at Kitty's involvement with her husband was the talk of London, and when the two women finally collided, sparks flew.

'The other day they ran into each other in the park,' said eyewitness Guistiana Wynne, Countess Rosenberg-Orsini, 'And Lady Coventry asked Kitty the name of the dressmaker who had made her dress. Kitty Fisher answered she had better ask Lord Coventry as he had given her the dress as a gift.' Kitty intended her comeback to sting and it did. Lady Coventry was furious and snapped back that Kitty was an impertinent woman. Kitty, of course, had plenty of experience of dealing with public altercations. Publicity was what had made her famous. She retorted that she had no choice but to accept Lady Coventry's insult, because Lady Coventry was her social superior. Maria should take heed though, warned Kitty, because she would marry a lord of her own, and then she would have every right to answer back.

In fact, Kitty never got her revenge. Lady Coventry died of lead poisoning at the age of 27, a victim of the Venetian ceruse she used to achieve her fashionably pale complexion. Kitty Fisher outlived her rival by less than a decade. After mere months of happy marriage to politician John Norris, she died in 1767, at the age of just 25.

A Whisper of Scandal: The Ladies of Bath

When author Sarah Robinson married George Lewis Scott, tutor to the future George III, he hadn't expected her to bring her best friend, Lady Barbara 'Bab' Montagu, along too. After the women eloped together for a new life of poverty-stricken philanthropy in Bath, rumours regarding the nature of their relationship were the talk of the town.

Miss Parsons' Ménage

In which a prime minister collides with a courtesan…

The name of Miss Parsons would hardly have been known, if the First Lord of the Treasury had not led her in triumph through the Opera House, even in the presence of the Queen. When we see a man act in this manner, we may admit the depravity of his heart, but what are we to think of his understanding?[1]

Augustus Henry FitzRoy, 3rd Duke of Grafton, seemed to have it all: titles, money and a political career that was in the ascendancy. He would eventually serve as prime minister of Great Britain and, like so many of his fellow First Lords of the Treasury, he was no stranger to scandal.

Grafton's wife was Anne Liddell, whom he married in 1756. Anne was the daughter of Baron Ravensworth and brought a dowry of thousands into her marriage. She lost no time in providing her husband with an heir and a spare, which seemed like the icing on the cake for the young, fashionable and eminently enviable couple. Yet looks can be deceiving.

With her husband focused on his political career and indulging his passions for horse racing, whoring and hunting in his spare time, Lady Grafton grew bored. She searched for some way to fill her days and soon discovered the dubious delights of gambling. Unfortunately, she didn't have much of a talent for it. Lady Anne's losses soon far exceeded her winnings, and her husband grew keen to put some distance between himself and his wife's spiralling debts. When she was pregnant with the couple's third child, Lord Grafton suddenly demanded a private

---

1. Anonymous (1783). The Letters of the Celebrated Junius, Vol I. London: Privately published, pp.113–114.

separation, much to Lady Anne's horror. She was blindsided when he ordered her out of the family home, with only one concession: though she could take her newborn daughter, she was compelled to leave her sons behind. Now Grafton went to town and he didn't care who knew it. It was one thing to take a mistress, but it was quite another to do so without the slightest suggestion of discretion. Yet that was exactly what the Duke of Grafton did.

Anne Parsons, who was known as *Nancy*, was the daughter of a tailor, but she was destined for much bigger things. Nancy had worked as a prostitute before making an ill-fated trip to Jamaica with a man who may or may not have become her husband. She used his name on her return, calling herself 'Mrs Horton' to provide a veneer of respectability even as she resumed her earlier profession.

Nancy became one of the most illustrious courtesans in London, and her list of clients positively glittered. In 1764 she began an affair with Lord Grafton, who was so besotted with her that he was happy to brush aside convention. Rather than show discretion when seeing Nancy, he did the exact opposite and she became a familiar fixture on her lover's arm. She lived openly in Grafton's home, but when he took her to the opera, where they allegedly enjoyed each other more than the show, and paraded her before the queen, polite society was scandalised.

By the time Grafton became prime minister, Nancy Parsons was his unofficial official hostess. He was mocked in the press for his infatuation and accused of neglecting his political and social duties to attend her. Just as kings' mistresses had brokered favours and sold promotions since time immemorial, so too could those of a senior politician. Nancy Parsons had become a very useful lady to know. It was to her that those seeking promotion applied, and the chattering classes were utterly scandalised.

'The happiest of her sex,' wrote *Town and Country Magazine*, 'attached to the most amiable man of the age, whose rank and influence raise her, in point of power, beyond many queens of the earth. Caressed by the highest, courted and adulated by all, her merit and shining abilities receive that applause that is justly due to them. She presides constantly at his sumptuous table, and does the honours with an ease and elegance, that the first nobility in the kingdom are compelled to admire.'

But the beleaguered Duchess of Grafton was no shrinking violet either. Banished by her husband, Anne wasn't about to fade into the background. When she fell pregnant by her lover, John FitzPatrick, 2nd Earl of Upper Ossory, in 1769, the hypocritical Duke of Grafton decided that enough was enough. He commenced divorce proceedings against his wife at precisely the same moment that his relationship with Nancy Parsons fell off the edge of a cliff. Had things turned out differently, the tailor's daughter might have ended up a duchess. Instead, Lord Grafton discovered that she had been sleeping with John Sackville, 3rd Duke of Dorset – but one wonders who wasn't. Never a man to take perceived betrayals lightly, Grafton ended the relationship and threw Nancy out.

The divorce made Lord Grafton the biggest scoundrel in England. He was nicknamed the Black Duke and the public called for his removal from office, arguing that he satisfied his own needs ahead of those of the country. Press criticism of Grafton was loud and vociferous, and he was constantly berated by the notorious and anonymous commentator Junius, whose loathing of Grafton knew no bounds. In the years to come, Parliament heard no less than four bills attempting to deal with the rise in crim con cases, as the perceived immorality of the upper classes battered England's belief in its so-called *betters*.

Three months after he had finalised his divorce and slung his mistress out on her ear, the Duke of Grafton married again. His bride this time was Elizabeth Wrottesley, who became mother to nine children by her husband. In divorcing Anne and marrying Elizabeth, Grafton became the first and only prime minister to divorce and remarry whilst in office, until Boris Johnson repeated the dubious feat.

And what of Anne and Nancy, the women in his life? Soon after her divorce, the disgraced former Duchess of Grafton married the 2nd Earl of Upper Ossory, the father of her illegitimate child. Nancy Parsons, meanwhile, indulged in just a little more scandal before her career came to an end. She retained her position as Dorset's mistress for several years, before moving on to Charles Maynard, 2nd Viscount Maynard, who proposed to her mere months after their affair began. Their marriage was just as infamous as everything else in this story, and the notorious pair found themselves shunned by the king and queen. Unbowed, Lord and Lady Maynard headed for the continent and entered in a ménage à trois with the teenaged Francis Russell, 5th Duke of Bedford, who was half the lady's age.

Surprisingly, that was one of the least shocking things Nancy ever did and the arrangement even had the support of the young man's grandmother. Better the scandalous couple you know, than the devil you don't.

A Whisper of Scandal: Too Much of a Good Thing

Anne Percy seemingly had it all. She was married to Hugh Percy, heir to the dukedom of Northumberland, and lived at the pinnacle of society. When her husband caught her in bed with a student, he sued for adultery, only to find himself ridiculed in the press, which argued that his love of masturbation and addiction to brothels had left his wife with little choice but to seek affection elsewhere.

Messalina and Lord Fumble

In which a countess refuses to be cowed and a New Female Coterie is born...

> Were we to give credit to the many reports circulated concerning her L—y—p's amours, to enumerate only the names of her gallants, would nearly fill the usual extent of this article. She has been represented of a disposition so very ambitious as well as amorous, that the world have ascribed to her a subordination of lovers from a monarch down to a hair-dresser; and, that every new member of the diplomatic body has constantly a private audience with her L—p, to present his credentials of love.[1]

In the Georgian era, a gentleman's worth, status and political colours were demonstrated by every decision he took in his life. Unlike his mother, wife, daughter or sister, society might turn a blind eye to a gentleman's most outrageous sexual extravagances, and he could still expect to be welcomed into White's or Brooks's, as long as his credit was good and he observed the social niceties of the day. Clubs for women were in considerably shorter supply, and considerably less tolerant too.

In 1769, William Almack, the noted club owner of Georgian London, formed a social society for 'ladies of quality'. The meetings would eventually be held at the famed Almack's Assembly Rooms and, though men were welcome to attend, the focus was clear from the name of the club: the Female Coterie. The members of the Coterie were some of the most senior women in England by social rank, and membership was by

---

1. Anonymous (1771). *The Town and Country Magazine, or Universal Repository of Knowledge, Instruction, and Entertainment.* London: A. Hamilton Jnr, p.12.

ballot. Women voted for male members and men for female members, meaning that no member could blackball a social rival out of sheer spite. Annual membership was 5 guineas, with meals and entertainments attracting an extra cost. This was not a club for the empty-pursed, though men alone were expected to foot the bill for wines enjoyed at lavish 8-guinea dinners.

'There is a new institution that begins to make, and if it proceeds, will make a considerable noise,' wrote Horace Walpole. 'It is a club of both sexes to be erected at Almack's, on the mode of that of the men of White's.'[2] And proceed it did. Within a year of being established, the society numbered 123 and could boast five dukes and a host of titled members. For those noblewomen who faced disgrace, however, membership was impossible. Regardless of how much money they boasted, the Female Coterie would not so much as consider allowing one of the tarnished demi-monde to attend its august meetings.

Caroline Stanhope, Countess of Harrington, was one such woman. Blackballed by the members of the Female Coterie, she decided that the only appropriate response was to establish her own rival group, which would welcome women who were supposedly damaged goods. The New Female Coterie was born. And it met in a brothel.

Caroline was the daughter of the 2nd Duke of Grafton and aunt to the notorious 3rd Duke. She was also the wife of William Stanhope, 2nd Earl of Harrington, whose wild reputation earned him the nicknames 'Lord Fumble' and 'the Goat of Quality'. Unlike other wives, who either bore their husband's betrayals with gritted teeth or embarked on their own secret romances, the Countess of Harrington gave as good as she got. Caroline was celebrated for her beauty and devotion to all things extra. She dripped in diamonds at the coronation of George III and courted infamy at every turn. With her voracious sexual appetite, it was difficult to avoid it.

The Earl and Countess of Harrington were perfectly well-matched, but whilst he sallied forth to the brothel of Sarah Pendergast, Lady

2. Anonymous (1837). *Correspondence of Horace Walpole with George Montague, Esq, Vol III*. London: Henry Colburn, p.2.

Harrington didn't stray too far from home in search of entertainment. The proximity of the couple's London house to the stables of St James's Park was a gift to the press, and, as Caroline's list of lovers grew, she earned the nickname of 'the Stable Yard Messalina'. It was a reference to both her home and a disrespectful nod to Empress Messalina. It was rumoured that Lady Harrington wasn't choosy about her partners either, and would happily take a lover from any strata of society. All that mattered was that she was having fun, and if *Town and Country* was to be believed, she was having fun with everyone from a northern potentate to her own domestic servants. Diplomatic staff, they noted, were a particular favourite of the insatiable countess.

Yet perhaps most shocking of all to the pearl-clutching members of high society was the fact that the Countess of Harrington didn't confine her affairs to men. She was bisexual, and in her youth had enjoyed a passionate and fiery affair – regarded as nothing more than intense friendship by contemporaries – with Elizabeth 'the Pollard'[3] Ashe, who eloped to marry Edward Wortley Montagu in 1751. Intriguingly, their tight-knit group of two occasionally became a trio, with Elizabeth and Caroline also enjoying an intimate friendship with Elizabeth Chudleigh, later the scandalous *Duchess-Countess*, in their youth.

The Countess of Harrington might have faced social rejection as a result of her unashamedly apologetic sex life, but she still had the safety net provided by money and privilege. When she was blackballed by the Female Coterie, she had two choices that a woman of lower social standing would not. She could withdraw into polite semi-retirement, enjoying her money and the social protection afforded by the fact that her husband, who was under no illusions about his own behaviour, would not contemplate divorce. That was the option that her more 'proper' contemporaries might have preferred. The other path was to do exactly as she was already doing and continue to live a life of unapologetic hedonism. This was the route that the Countess of Harrington chose.

Denied access to the Female Coterie, Lady Caroline formed the New Female Coterie instead. It held its meetings in the brothel owned by

---

3. Horace Walpole liked to remind his correspondents of this nickname.

Mrs Pendergast, which was one of Lord Harrington's favourite places to spend his money. For Mrs Pendergast, it was a splendid turn of events – now her establishment could boast some of the grandest and most notorious names in the land. And with their agreement, she was even able to offer their services to her more select clients.

Lady Caroline was joined in her club by a host of scandalous and fallen gentlewomen. Among them were Lady Grosvenor, the Honourable Catherine Newton; Penelope, Viscountess Ligonier; and Seymour Dorothy Fleming, the notorious Lady Worsley.

Lady Catherine had caused a scandal when she married John Newton at the age of 16. He was more than forty years her senior and was soon horrified to find himself openly cuckolded by members of his own household. Their marriage ended in divorce. Viscountess Ligonier was no stranger to gossip either, and she too had been a 16-year-old bride to an older man, whose passion for his horses and military career far exceeded that he had for his wife. Her liaisons with the Italian Count Vittorio Alfieri ended in a duel that took place in 1771. When the two men met in Green Park, Viscount Ligonier claimed the victory and Alfieri was lucky to escape with his life. The couple's highly-publicised divorce threatened to ruin Penelope completely, but she was determined not to be the victim. Instead, she wrote openly of her affair and admitted that she didn't regret it for a second. Her marriage was loveless and entirely devoid of passion, something she had finally experienced with her Italian lover. If ruin was the price of freedom, she was happy to pay it.

Perhaps most scandalous of all was Lady Worsley, the immensely wealthy woman who supposedly had over two dozen lovers. Her marriage to Sir Richard Worsley, 7th Baronet, collapsed in 1782 amid accusations of adultery. Yet Lady Worsley fought back against her husband's criminal conversation case and produced a host of witnesses who were happy to confirm that he had cuckolded her innumerable times. He had infected Lady Worsley with venereal disease and treated his wife as a piece of property to be displayed and disregarded. The jury bridled at Worsley's depravity and awarded him just 1 shilling in damages, a far cry from the £20,000 he had been hoping for from Maurice George Bisset, who had fathered a child with Lady Worsley which her husband claimed as his own.

The members of the New Female Coterie used their monthly gatherings to discuss whatever took their fancy, and they took full advantage of the opportunities offered by their headquarters. They didn't hold their meetings in a brothel by accident and were able to supplement their income by taking their pick of the wealthiest and most appealing patrons of Mrs Pendergast's house. Legend has it that Viscountess Ligonier had slept with her own former husband at a masked ball, revealing her identity only once she was sure that she had given him a dose of something suitably unpleasant.

All would have been well had it not been for the Earl of Harrington, who found that daily visits to the brothel soon meant that he had exhausted his pick of the women on offer. He asked Sarah Pendergast to gather some new candidates, and she hired Country Bet and Black Susan, two sex workers from the house of a Mother Butler. After several hours in their company, Lord Harrington tried his luck and attempted to palm the women off with 3 guineas each, a vast underpayment. Even worse, 25 per cent of that would be due to Mother Butler, and 25 per cent of 6 guineas just wouldn't cut it.

Mother Butler accused the women of trying to con her and demanded their finest gowns in recompense. When they reported her for stealing, the messy matter ended up in court and, inevitably, in the papers. It was one thing to visit a brothel four times a week for a threesome, but it was another to see that splashed across the headlines, and the earl tried to buy up every single newspaper that mentioned his name. He demanded that Mrs Pendergast lend a hand and she sent out half a dozen girls to grab every paper they could. Mindful of just how much cash Earl Harrington spent in her establishment, Mrs Pendergast also paid Country Bet and Black Susan 5 guineas each to retract their claims and drop the court case. On top of that, she had to assure her clients that she could guarantee their anonymity should they continue to frequent her brothel.

Lord Harrington had been left depressed by the court case and his public ribbing, but when he received Mrs Pendergast's report, he hurried to an audience with her. Joyous at the news of her success, he had the newspapers thrown on a bonfire and bought porter for all the lady's neighbours. 'Many people thought that some important good news had arrived,' wrote one wag. 'That we had either completely defeated Washington or taken D'Orvillier's whole fleet.[4] But it was a little more earthy than that.

Mother Pendergast saved her business by the skin of her teeth, and the Earl of Harrington learned nothing. He was a four-times a week man, after all.

---

4. Anonymous (1779). *Nocturnal Revels, Vol II*, London: M. Goadby, p.204.

Lady Derby and the Duke of Dorset

In which a Countess learns the cost of scandal…

[The Duke of Dorset] is waiting for a Duchess till Lady Derby is divorced. He would not marry her before Lord Derby did and now is forced to take her, when he himself has made her a very bad match. A quarter of our Peeresses will have been wives of half our living Peers.[1]

Life in the Georgian era could be a curious mix of moral outrage and blind eyes turned. It won't come as any surprise to learn that when the battlelines of the genders were drawn, all too often it was the woman who emerged on the backfoot should scandal envelope a marriage. A quick look at some of the realities of the marriage market – for even the richest and most privileged woman – might come as something of an eyeopener. It wasn't all assembly rooms and heated glances over the punchbowl.

Some of the women who figured in the greatest scandals of the Georgian era were fabulously wealthy, but that wealth existed only as long as they were single. Even then, it was a means by which to attract a husband, and often not one the bride got to choose. Upon marriage, that fortune – the bride's dowry – was surrendered to her new spouse, who would then decide how much, if any, would be his wife's to spend as she wished. Many marriages were made for social and dynastic reasons rather than love, and some men were past masters at pantomiming affection until the dowry was in their hands. Domestic violence was

---

1. Walpole, Horace (1844). *Letters of Horace Walpole, Earl of Orford, to Sir Horace Mann, Vol II*. Philadelphia: Lea & Blanchard, p.88.

widely tolerated and even legal, under the understanding that the male head of a household could dole out moderate correction to those who lived under his authority. Today this is unthinkable, and in the eighteenth century, the line between moderate and excessive was open to wide interpretation.

Should a woman eventually decide to leave her husband, the chance of her seeing her children again was virtually nil unless he allowed it. Even George I, who had fathered three illegitimate daughters with his mistress, punished his former wife for adultery by denying her the right to see her children for the last thirty years of her life. And whilst the likes of King George were divorcing their wives and pursuing romances left, right and centre, no such possibility existed for women. They had no right to sue for divorce or separation. If they chose to leave their husband for any reason, the law was not there to support them. In many cases, they had little choice but to take up with another man, who would become their keeper and, they hoped, their protector.

One such woman was Elizabeth Smith-Stanley, Countess of Derby. Known as *Betty*, Lady Derby was the daughter of James Hamilton, 6th Duke of Hamilton, and his wife Elizabeth, the second of the celebrated Gunning sisters. Betty 'had the figure of a sylph, the air and step of a Hebe,' wrote her sister, Lady Charlotte Campbell, who sadly found her 'an easy prey to folly and vice.'[2] The young Lady Betty was soon one of the most eligible girls in the land and the battle for her hand was fierce. Amongst the keenest players was William Cavendish, the fashionable and influential 5th Duke of Devonshire, who paid court to Elizabeth with such fervent admiration that all of polite society was certain that the couple would be married.

Fate, however, had a different idea. Lady Betty had enchanted two other men. One was John Sackville, 3rd Duke of Dorset – later the man who ended Nancy Parsons' chances of becoming a duchess – and the other, a fellow named Nisbet, who was so besotted by Lady Betty that he travelled to Italy to seek her brother's permission to marry. It was

---

2. Stokes, Hugh (1917). *The Devonshire House Circle*. London: Herbert Jenkins Limited, p.61.

Dorset that Lady Betty really wanted, but the womanising duke had plenty of other irons in the fire. He thought nothing of leaving England to pursue business abroad, thus denying the young woman the proposal she had hoped for. Whilst Elizabeth was intriguing with Nisbet, and Dorset was out of the picture, the Duke of Devonshire moved on and became betrothed to his celebrated wife, Georgiana. Poor Mr Nisbet, meanwhile, was no match for the empire-building ways of Lady Betty's family, and a marriage was brokered between the young lady and the hugely wealthy Edward Smith-Stanley, heir to the Earldom of Derby. The future Lord Derby was determined to woo Lady Betty, but as Lady Charlotte Campbell remembered, 'Lord Derby's constant and assiduous care veiled the ugliness of his person before the idol he worshipped.'[3] The opulent parties he threw in Lady Elizabeth's honour failed to charm her, but they worked their magic on her family. With little choice, a sobbing Lady Elizabeth consented to the marriage. 'No blandishments that power and passion could bestow were spared to dazzle the unhappy victim,'[4] sighed her sister.

A fortune had already been spent on the forthcoming wedding when the Duke of Dorset returned to England. His reappearance shattered Lady Betty because it had come just a little too late and there could be no going back. The wedding she had begun to dread went ahead in June 1774. Elizabeth was 21, her husband a year her senior; his passions were horse racing and cockfighting, and his fortune was what had recommended him to Lady Betty's family. She would come to rue their decision.

In the following years, Elizabeth gave birth to three children by her husband, but she was far from satisfied with her match. When Edward became Earl of Derby in 1776, his wife was considered one of the most beautiful and accomplished women in the land, yet she longed for something more. Lady Betty's fleeting intrigue with the Duke of Dorset had not gone away when he returned to his travels, but deepened. Now the infamous rake was home, the Countess of Derby could think of

3. Ibid., p.69.
4. Ibid., p.70.

nothing but him. The couple began an affair, but if they hoped to keep it quiet, they were to be disappointed. The Countess of Derby and the Duke of Dorset were soon the talk of the town.

If ever there was proof of the opposing manner in which women and men were treated when it came to scandal, this case was it. With the press and pamphleteers making great capital of the affair, Lady Derby took a calculated gamble and left her husband. She went to ground in the countryside, ostracised by polite society even though Derby and Dorset continued as friends. Still Betty was certain that she could weather the storm, safe in the knowledge that it was simply a matter of time before her husband sued for divorce. Once she was free, Betty reasoned that Dorset would marry her and she would return to society, triumphant in the robes of a duchess. Instead, Derby refused to grant her wish for a divorce, and the law did not allow her to initiate proceedings herself.

The impact was devastating. Although many women privately felt much sympathy for the countess, she was effectively a pariah, denied access to her children and refused admittance to the society and friends she had once enjoyed. Yet Betty still clung to her passion for the inconstant Duke of Dorset, as more and more doors were slammed shut in her face. Perhaps her greatest social embarrassment came when Queen Charlotte herself rejected the possibility of welcoming the disgraced countess at court. Had she done so, polite society would surely have rallied behind Lady Betty, but the pious and proper Charlotte was adamant. Until the Earl and Countess of Derby were reunited, Lady Betty would not be welcome at court.

When Dorset also spurned her, Lady Betty was broken. Her health failed and she fled to the continent where she lived a restless, unsettled life. Meanwhile, at home, Lord Derby was reaping the rewards of his pig-headed refusal to free his wife. He had developed a passion for the actress Elizabeth Farren, but she refused to become his mistress. He couldn't even hope for a few minutes alone with her, since Miss Farren always requested her mother join them as a chaperone for the sake of her reputation. Society talked of nothing but his fruitless attempts to woo Elizabeth Farren, mocking the would-be Casanova who was permanently frustrated by his paramour's morals and mother.

When Lady Betty returned to England, it was not to the glittering lifestyle she had once enjoyed, but her life was lonely no longer. She was seen out in society with the fashionable Duchess of Devonshire, who had once described the rakish Duke of Dorset as 'the most dangerous of men', and kept her head held high when Dorset, the man for whom she had lost everything, married another. Lady Betty found friendship with like-minded and similarly disgraced women as a member of the New Female Coterie, a place where she might finally be regarded as more than the headline-grabbing scandals that had nearly ruined her.

The Countess of Derby died in 1797. Six weeks later, the widowed Earl of Derby finally got his wish and married Elizabeth Farren. Presumably, there would no longer be any need for a chaperone.

A Whisper of Scandal: Say Cheese

The Marquis of Blandford told his married lover, Lady Mary Anne Sturt, that he'd give up everything if she would agree to elope with him. Instead, her husband sued him, and the press revelled in stories of love letters hidden in wheels of Parmesan… a cheesy trick indeed.

The Hunter and the Sailor

In which a royal favourite elopes with a favourite of his own...

> Husbands are dreadfull [*sic*] and powerful Animals. I have a most constant headache at present, from what I have gone through about it all.[1]

As the Countess of Derby learned to her cost, should a woman be seen to have abandoned her husband in Georgian Britain, the price could be high. So long as that husband refused to take her back or seek the divorce that would allow her to wed another, she was effectively in limbo. Though Lady Derby eventually managed a rehabilitation of sorts, after years spent flitting around Europe and the English countryside, the life she had once known was denied to her. It was a miserable fate, but one that only women faced. Just as the Earl of Derby continued to socialise with the Duke of Dorset, even after the latter fuelled the breakdown of the Derbys' marriage, a husband who abandoned his bride also faced little censure from society. He faced little consequence, too, since his wronged wife had no right to sue for divorce or separation. All she could do was square her shoulders and try to weather the storm with dignity.

One woman who knew all about this was Lady Elizabeth Spencer, the daughter of the Duke of Marlborough. She was just 19 when she married Henry Herbert, 10th Earl of Pembroke, and would not be the only Spencer sister who became hitched to a deadweight of a husband. Yet, at first, all seemed to be going well. The Pembrokes' first child was born three years after their marriage, but in the seventeen years before

---

1. Hicks, Carola (2002). *Improper Pursuits: The Scandalous Life of an Earlier Lady Diana Spencer*. New York: St Martin's Press, p.253.

their second child came along, Lord and Lady Pembroke packed in a lifetime's worth of scandal.

The young couple was part of England's social elite and, to the outside, their life must have looked ideal. Rich, decorated and seemingly possessed of a Midas touch, Lord Pembroke was a celebrated soldier and one of George III's Lords of the Bedchamber, whilst Lady Pembroke served as Lady of the Bedchamber to Queen Charlotte. With a country seat at Wilton House and a fashionable London address at their disposal during the season, few could've guessed what was to come. Lady Pembroke certainly had no inkling.

Elizabeth Catherine Hunter, meanwhile, occupied a sphere some way from that of the glittering Pembrokes. Born in 1740, she was six years the Earl of Pembroke's junior, and three years younger than his wife. She was the daughter of politician Thomas Orby Hunter, who served as a Lord of the Admiralty, and she was known to one and all as *Kitty*. Kitty Hunter was a maid of honour to Queen Charlotte and had already begun to make a little splash at the royal court, but nobody admired her as much as Lord Pembroke. Soon their flirtations were out of control, and Lord Pembroke began to hatch a plan.

Early in 1762, Kitty and Pembroke shared a dance at a masked ball. As they took a turn on the floor, the couple revelled in a shared secret. That night, they were merely two costumed courtiers, but within hours they would be the talk of the town. Perhaps ironically, Joshua Reynolds was painting portraits of both Lady Pembroke and Kitty Hunter as the latter was planning to elope with the husband of the former. The finished painting of Kitty shows her at the very masked ball where she decided her fate.

The following day, Lord Pembroke had arranged for a party of his wife's family and friends to visit the family home for dinner. As the hour approached, he sent his apologies and explained that he must attend to urgent business elsewhere. Then, as Lady Pembroke prepared to greet her visitors alone, he secretly dressed in the outfit of a sailor and donned a black wig to conceal his identity. Lord Pembroke left a letter for his wife in which he begged her not to write to him unless she wanted to break his heart. In the same letter, he asked her to implore the king not to strip him of his rank of Major General. Then, as the evening drew on, Lord Pembroke slipped away.

The runaway earl and Kitty Hunter fled England together aboard a packet boat that was headed for Europe. They left behind a heartbroken and bewildered Lady Pembroke, who had been unfailingly loyal to her husband. She had not expected him to be anything but loving and devoted in return.

> Lord Pembroke, Earl, Lord of the Bedchamber, Major-General, possessed of ten thousand pounds a year, Master of Wilton, husband of one of the most beautiful creatures in England, father of an only son, and himself but eight-and-twenty to enjoy this assemblage of good fortune, is gone off with Miss Hunter, daughter to one of the Lords of the Admiralty, a handsome girl with a fine person, but silly and in no degree lovely as his own wife, who has the face of a Madonna, and, with all the modesty of that idea, is doatingly fond of him. He left letters resigning all his employments, and one to witness to the virtue of Lady Pembroke, whom he says he has long tried in vain to make hate and dislike him. It is not yet known whither this foolish guilty couple have bent their course; but you may imagine the distress of the earl's family, and the resentment of the house of Marlborough, who doat on their sister: Miss Helen's family too takes it for no honour. Her story is not so uncommon; but did one ever hear of an earl running away from himself?[2]

Lord Pembroke and Kitty Hunter were effectively on the run, hurtling through the Low Countries much to the amusement of society gossips and the fury of Kitty's father. Horace Walpole, of course, lapped it up; the affair even drove him to poetry:

> As Pembroke a horseman by most is accounted,
> 'Tis not strange that his Lordship a Hunter has mounted.

---

2. Walpole, Horace (1843). *Letters of Horace Walpole, Earl of Orford, to Sir Horace Mann, Vol I*. London: Richard Bentley, pp.71–72.

Lady Pembroke was distraught, but things were only going to get worse. The Earl of Pembroke wanted to have it all, and as he partied with his young mistress on the continent, he longed to be reunited with his heartbroken wife. She longed for him too and was still willing to forgive her errant spouse if he agreed to give up Kitty and come home. But Lord Pembroke didn't want one woman or the other – he wanted both. What better, he decided, than to propose a ménage à trois?

Lord Pembroke wrote to Elizabeth and suggested that she should come to Utrecht and join him and Kitty. 'He must be mad,' wrote her friend, Caroline Fox, echoing the prevailing mood. Lady Pembroke, needless to say, did not go to Utrecht, and within a month of their flight, Pembroke and Kitty's elopement was at an end. The couple was discovered aboard a boat in the North Sea by a privateer who had previously worked for Kitty's father, and Kitty was brought back to England. Pembroke gave chase in a fishing boat, determined not to be parted from his paramour, but it was hardly a dashing white charger. By now Kitty was pregnant and her father turned the couple away, saying that he didn't actually want his daughter back at all. As far as he was concerned, she had become a liability.

Once more the couple invited Lady Pembroke to join them on their adventures, and though she was tempted by love for her thoughtless husband, once more she refused. Pembroke and Kitty headed for Europe again, where Lord Pembroke dispatched endless love letters to his wife, begging the heartbroken woman for money as his infamy faded. Lord Pembroke couldn't stay on the run forever, and when he was recalled to his regiment, he wrote to Lady Pembroke and admitted that he was considering a trip to England to seek her forgiveness before he went into battle. This time the heartbroken woman showed a little more spirit and warned him that he had better not think of showing his face unless he was coming home to stay.

The return to military duty seemed to be just what Lord Pembroke needed to clear his head and realise what he really wanted. And what he wanted would break another woman's heart. When his tour ended this time, he headed for England and a reconciliation with his wife. Kitty's father grudgingly agreed to take Kitty back if she would return the settlement Pembroke had given her and give up her child. She agreed to hand back the money, but she would not abandon her son.[3] In the event, Kitty was wily enough to keep both, along with an allowance from Pembroke for the next twenty years. When the Pembrokes offered to let the child take their family name, however, it was Lady Pembroke who vetoed the idea. Instead, he would be known as Montgomery, in recognition of his father's secondary title of 8th Earl of Montgomery.

One might think that Pembroke had learned his lesson, but he had simply learned that he could get away with anything. In 1768 he fathered an illegitimate child with a woman he seduced on the eve of her wedding, but this time there was no elopement. Years later, when the Pembrokes' 10-year-old daughter fell ill with consumption, the couple took her to France to take the medicinal waters, but Pembroke had other things on his mind. He left his wife and dying child, and absconded to Italy with a comely dancer, but soon returned to his countess. Lord Pembroke had learned the value of discretion, if nothing else. Kitty Hunter went on to marry, and the Pembrokes continued their respective military and court careers. The scandals were behind them, and in Georgian high society, money and title were quick routes to forgiveness... so long as you were a man.

---

3. They named the child Augustus Retnuh Reebkomp; his second name was Hunter written backwards, his surname an anagram of Pembroke. Understandably, he preferred to be known by the surname Montgomery.

Bully the Battersea Baron

In which Lady Diana Spencer is most cruelly used…

> The affair of Lord and Lady Bolingbroke is likely to become very serious, and a great amusement to the town when it fills, according as people's curiosity or sensibility is the most predominant. The *Chronique* says she is brought to bed. Servants are become evidencers, and the husband hopes by this imprudent management of her and her simple lover, to be freed a vinculo matrimonii, and in future times to marry a rich monster and retrieve his affairs. I hope you will not quote me.[1]

When George Selwyn, himself rumoured to have a penchant for necrophilia, warned Lord Holland to expect scandal courtesy of *The Morning Chronicle* in August 1767, he pre-empted one of the hottest talking points in London that season. Through no fault of her own, Viscountess Bolingbroke was about to become big news.

Known to all as Lady Di, Viscountess Bolingbroke had been born Lady Diana Spencer. Her sister was Elizabeth, who made such an unhappy match to the errant Lord Pembroke, and Lady Di's marriage was to be no happier than that of her sibling. The Spencers were a powerful and wealthy family, meaning that Diana and Elizabeth were two of the most eligible women in the land, and eminently well connected too. Lady Di was a personal favourite of Queen Charlotte, to whom she was Lady of the Bedchamber, and the family was a fixture at the St James's court of

---

1. Fox, Henry, & Fox-Strangeways, Stephen, Earl of Ilchester (1915). *Letters to Henry Fox, Lord Holland, With a Few Addressed to His Brother, Stephen, Earl of Ilchester.* London: The Roxburgh Club, p.280.

King George III. Men set out to woo the sisters not because of love, but because of the influence that marriage into the House of Marlborough could bring. The enormous dowries waiting for the successful suitors didn't do any harm either.

It certainly wasn't love that caused Frederick St John, 2nd Viscount Bolingbroke, to pursue Lady Di. Known as Bully to his contemporaries, he lived a life of extravagance and pleasure, spending a fortune on his passion for women, drinking and breeding racehorses. Bolingbroke had already romanced Lady Coventry, who went to war with Kitty Fisher, and he considered that snaring Lady Di would be a pushover.

Of course, Bully was right. Though his reputation was anything but whiter than white, his pedigree was undeniable. Just a couple of generations earlier, Bully's family name had been notorious thanks to the shenanigans of his uncle, the 1st Viscount Bolingbroke, who fled for France amid accusations of treason against George I. By the reign of the third King George, though, all of that was behind them. Meanwhile, despite the handsome dowries attached to the Duke of Marlborough's daughters, that illustrious family was not as rich as it had once been. It was perhaps inevitable that when the wealthy Bully jokingly proposed to Lady Di during a heady night at Vauxhall Pleasure Gardens, what started as a prank soon turned serious.

The couple were wed in 1757, but despite the swift arrival of three children, things were far from happy. Bully continued his bachelor lifestyle, even resuming his affair with Maria, Countess of Coventry, and he frittered away Lady Di's dowry at White's and Newmarket, caring nothing for the wife he left sitting at home. He wasn't satisfied with his mistress either and was a familiar sight at the capital's brothels, even infecting the humiliated Lady Di on more than one occasion. Many years later, a wag of a journalist suggested that Bully had deliberately infected his wife, hoping she would pass the disease to any future lovers. Something had to give.

Topham Beauclerk was a gentleman of fashion. According to legend, he was the illegitimate great-grandson of Nell Gwyn and Charles II, and he had romance in his veins. A lover of art who had travelled in Europe and now belonged to a circle of literary wits that included

Horace Walpole and Samuel Johnson, Beauclerk and Lady Di had more in common than anyone might have guessed. They both moved in fashionable circles, she a Lady of the Bedchamber to Queen Charlotte, he a young Macaroni about town, and their mutual attraction was impossible to resist.

Swept along on a heady cloud of romance, Lady Di did the unthinkable. Unlike so many of her contemporaries, she didn't pursue a secret affair whilst maintaining her miserable marriage. Instead, she left the marital home and went to stay first with her brother. She then moved into a home of her own, where she went out of her way to give the impression that hers was a virtually monastic life. In reality, she was secretly enjoying long, uninterrupted liaisons with Topham Beauclerk. Bully, who one might reasonably accuse of having contributed to his own heartbreak, was ruing the decisions that had led him to the single life. 'I am so low, dejected, and miserable, that I cannot speak; I can only cry,' he told George Selwyn, 'If you ever happen to talk of me to Lady Di, represent me as appearing to you altered and unhappy.'[2]

As we know, secrets were hard to keep in Georgian London. The houses of the wealthy were run like clockwork by an army of domestic staff, and though many were fiercely loyal, some were not. It's human nature to gossip and the servants at Lady Di's house were no different, especially when Beauclerk became a regular overnight guest, sleeping either in a room adjoining that of his hostess, or sharing her bed. The situation was ripe for blackmail, and the first person to exploit it was Lady Di's footman, William Flockton. Flockton had walked in on the couple *in flagrante* in the dining room, and extorted a handsome sum in return for his silence, but it was perhaps inevitable that he wouldn't be satisfied with a one-off payment. Flockton knew everything that happened in the home of the separated viscountess, and the more Beauclerk behaved as though he was master, the more resentful the footman became. Even Samuel Johnson weighed in, declaring: 'The woman's a whore and there's an end on't.'

2. Jesse, John Heneage (1843). *George Selwyn and His Contemporaries, Vol II*. London: Richard Bentley, p.78.

By January 1767, it seemed as though Lady Di could no longer conceal the affair. She had fallen pregnant by Beauclerk and, despite taking every effort to hide her condition beneath loosened stays and behind the secluded walls of her winter home at Taplow, rumours of the affair began to seep out. Flockton was dismissed, along with other gossiping members of the household, but when a little girl was born in August, it was obvious that the secret couldn't be maintained. News of the birth leaked into the press, and Bully learned with horror that his wife hadn't been living the quiet life he had been led to believe.

Bully brought a case of criminal conversation against Topham Beauclerk. As you might imagine, it was all very one-sided indeed. No mention was made of Bully's frequent philandering – though it was certainly no secret – and nobody so much as uttered the word *brothel*. Instead, the trial heard tell of dirty footprints on Lady Di's couch, as well as rumpled sheets, disordered cushions and all sorts of saucy sounds being heard from behind locked doors. Bully and Lady Di had worked it all out beforehand, coming to an agreement that he would not seek monetary damages if she would agree not to bring a counterclaim, thus ensuring that their parliamentary divorce would be a matter of routine. Nobody wanted to prolong the inevitable, least of all Bully. He knew full well that he stood to lose a substantial sum should a countersuit that revealed his own sexual escapades rumble on and on.

The divorce was finalised at Westminster in March 1768, making Bolingbroke only the fifth peer in history to divorce. Two days later, Lady Di and Beauclerk were married. Their family grew to three children and Lady Di, who had been dismissed from her position in the queen's household because of her notoriety, discovered a new career as an artist, including a stint designing pottery for Wedgwood. The Bolingbroke marriage became a byword for scandal, and the press milked it for all it was worth for years.

Lord Bolingbroke died in 1787, robbed of his wits by syphilis. His friends maintained that Bolingbroke's spirits had been broken by Lady Di's desertion, but her own life was no fairy tale. Beauclerk, once so fashionable, witty and celebrated, became increasingly reclusive and miserable as the years passed. Lady Di escaped into her artworks, but the family seemed to have a habit of getting themselves into trouble. When Lady Di's daughter, Mary, had a long relationship with her own half-brother – of which, more anon – the tale of the Bolingbrokes came hurtling back into the public eye. Scandal, as Lady Di learned, was never dead, merely sleeping.

A Whisper of Scandal: A Merry Ménage

Lady Georgiana Cavendish, the celebrated and fabulous Duchess of Devonshire, enjoyed a 25-year ménage à trois with her husband, the 5th Duke of Devonshire, and her best friend, Lady Elizabeth Foster. When Georgiana died, Bess kept it in the family and married the duke herself.

The Bigamous Bride

In which the Duchess of Kingston has one too many husbands…

The duchess was presumptuous, vain, imperious, and passionate.
— In the height of pride and insolence, she would often compare
herself to Juno. — She was ostentatious to excess, yet meanly
avaricious and cunning; and a dupe to the grossest flattery.

Connected with such a woman, it cannot be supposed that such
a man as the Duke of Kingston could enjoy connubial happiness,
but his duchess had so fascinated his mind, and obtained
such despotic sway over his reason, as enabled her to turn his
understanding to every measure her passions, inclinations, or
caprice dictated.[1]

The hottest ticket in 1776 wasn't for any theatrical extravaganza, but for
the House of Lords where bigamy charges against Elizabeth Chudleigh
were the business of the hour. The *Duchess-Countess*, as Horace Walpole
termed her, had always been an adventuress, and now it seemed as though
her wild life was about to catch up with her. Yet what led Elizabeth to
infamy, and what was her life once the spectators went home and the
Lords returned to less exciting business?

Though she eventually found a place in the royal household, Elizabeth
Chudleigh didn't come from the most illustrious stock. Like so many of
our other leading ladies, she was born to humble origins as the daughter
of a family who had pedigree, but little material wealth. Her father had
invested what money he possessed in South Sea stock and when the

---

1. Anonymous (1788). *The Life and Memoirs of Elizabeth Chudleigh, Afterwards Mrs Hervey and Countess of Bristol*. London: R. Randall, p.12.

bubble burst, it took his cash with it. He died when Elizabeth was just 5, leaving the family in deep water.

Luckily Elizabeth's mother was just as enterprising as her daughter would later prove to be. She took in lodgers to bolster her income and sent Elizabeth off to live in the country, where the little girl caught the eye of William Pulteney, 1st Earl of Bath. Lord Bath took Elizabeth under his supposedly platonic wing and brought her to London, where he was sure that her wit and intelligence would more than make up for her lack of formal education. Essentially, he was training her to embark on life in society; you may deduce his motives for yourself. Once he was sure Elizabeth was ready, Lord Bath used his influence to secure the 22-year-old beauty a position as a maid of honour to George III's mother, Augusta, Princess of Wales. At the royal court, Elizabeth made an instant and sparkling splash. Her intimate friendship with Elizabeth Ashe and Caroline, Countess of Harrington, only added to her allure.

Though Elizabeth had good looks and charm to spare, she knew that plenty of other young ladies at court could also boast those qualifications. What she had that they didn't was an acute understanding of the power of celebrity, and she knew that there was no better way to grab the limelight than behaving badly. When Elizabeth's dazzling conversation and comely beauty failed to grab attention, she resorted to clowning. One of her favourite tricks was to fart loudly at the dinner table, then pantomime horror and blame it on the dogs who were waiting for scraps.

Two years and several farts after she arrived at court, Elizabeth met the younger brother of the Earl of Bristol at Winchester races. It was love at first sight. Augustus John Hervey was a naval officer, but his brother's health was poor so he expected to one day inherit the title. At 20, he was three years Elizabeth's junior, and his £50 salary was only a quarter of hers, but the couple embarked on a whirlwind romance despite Hervey's imminent departure for a two-year tour of duty. Rather than bide their time and wait to see if the Earl of Bristol's health turned the corner, the couple was secretly married by moonlight in Lainston in Wiltshire on 4 August 1744. It was the stuff of romantic fiction, but there was no happy ending on the cards.

If word got out that Elizabeth was married, she would lose her position as a maid of honour, so she and Hervey agreed to keep their wedding a secret. When the groom departed for his two-year tour just a couple of days later, nobody was any the wiser. And Elizabeth was still Elizabeth.

Whilst her husband was away, the new Mrs Hervey didn't sit and pine. Instead, she got busy making herself popular and was romanced by both the Duke of Ancaster and the 6th Duke of Hamilton. Once she encountered their ducal charms, those of Augustus Hervey seemed rather dismal, and Elizabeth realised that she had made a serious error. She would have dearly loved to become the Duchess of Hamilton, but it wasn't to be. It *couldn't* be, though she could never tell him why. Instead, Hamilton wed Elizabeth Gunning, and became father to the scandalous Lady Betty, Countess of Derby.

By the time Hervey returned to England, Elizabeth had moved on from her heady summertime romance, and her husband too. She refused to see him, employing all manner of excuses to keep Hervey at bay until he despaired of ever setting eyes on his wife again. Eventually, Hervey warned that unless Elizabeth would visit him in his lodgings, he would make their secret marriage public. Elizabeth acquiesced grudgingly, only to find herself entrapped. According to reports that emerged later, Hervey raped Elizabeth and she fell pregnant with a baby boy who lived only a short time.

Terrorised, abused and filled with regret for her hasty marriage, Elizabeth could see no way out. On top of that, her once-secure position at court was looking distinctly wobbly. Elizabeth's wild ways were no longer considered charming, and she had acquired a reputation as a loose cannon whose bad behaviour was turning off more would-be husbands with every passing year. When she showed up at a masquerade ball in 1747 wearing a figure-hugging catsuit of flesh-coloured silk and a fig leaf, the court was aghast. George II, however, was delighted. He asked Elizabeth if he could touch her breast, but she replied sweetly that she could think of an even softer place where he might place his hand. When the lecherous king asked her to show him where that might be, Elizabeth took hold of his hand and placed it atop his own head. To everyone's surprise, the king fell about in amusement. It was a turning point in Elizabeth's career at court. Should she wish to become a royal mistress, the road lay open to her, but royal mistresses – particularly at the court of George II – had precious little security. Elizabeth wanted a new husband.

She met her perfect match in the handsome shape of Evelyn Pierrepont, 2nd Duke of Kingston-upon-Hull. Kingston was celebrated for his good looks and unshowy manner, and soon he and Elizabeth were inseparable. They travelled together in Europe, where Elizabeth beguiled Frederick the Great and shone at social occasions. In 1769, after many happy years together, the couple announced their plans to marry.

All of this would have been a perfect place to leave Elizabeth, if not for the thorny question of that other husband. Hervey would happily have divorced her, but a divorce would mean that the secret marriage would become public knowledge, and Kingston might have baulked at the idea of a divorcee for a duchess. When Hervey pressed the matter, Elizabeth came back swinging. She swore that she had never been legally married at all, and challenged Hervey to prove otherwise. The whole business washed up in court, where Hervey was once again told to produce evidence of the marriage. When he was unable to do so, the court found 'that the said Elizabeth Chudleigh was and now is a Spinster, and free from all matrimonial contracts and espousals with the said Augustus John Hervey.'[2] A few weeks later, the star-crossed lovers were married. Elizabeth Chudleigh was now the Duchess of Kingston-upon-Hull.

The Consistory Court was the only place that was convinced there had been no earlier marriage, though. Elizabeth's fellow courtiers echoed the opinion of polite society, who believed without a doubt that she was married to Hervey and was now a barefaced bigamist. Though Elizabeth had been accepted as the mistress of the Duke of Kingston-upon-Hull, when she became his bigamous bride, she was shunned. Yet her loving husband didn't care, and neither did she. The couple were

---

2. Anonymous (1794). *The Lawyer's and Magistrate's Magazine, Vol III for the Year MDCCXCI*. London: W. Jones, p.146.

blissfully happy together and enjoyed a peaceful, rural life away from the glare of society for several years until the duke's health began to fail. He died in 1773, leaving everything to his duchess on the strict condition that she did not marry again.

With the death of the duke, everything changed for Elizabeth. She found herself besieged by members of her late husband's family, all of whom were determined to challenge the legality of both the couple's marriage and the duke's will in the hope of getting their slice of a very rich pie indeed. Eventually, she fled England for Europe, where she was received not as a bigamous harlot, but with all the courtesy a duchess might expect. To make things even more tangled, just two years after she was widowed, Elizabeth's first husband succeeded his brother as Earl of Bristol. Elizabeth was now, as Horace Walpole noted with delight, the *Duchess-Countess*.

When the Duke of Kingston's nephew, Evelyn Meadows, launched legal proceedings against Elizabeth late in 1775, she had no choice but to return to England to fight her case. Meadows argued that the court had been wrong when it found that Elizabeth was not married to Hervey, and requested that the verdict be set aside, along with the will that left everything to Elizabeth Chudleigh. The case became headline news, and Samuel Foote even devised a play titled *A Trip to Calais*, in which a character named Kitty Crocodile served as a thinly-veiled caricature of the Duchess of Kingston. When Foote visited Elizabeth's home and asked for £2,000 to pull the planned premiere, she had the Lord Chamberlain ban the play outright. Foote went to the press, and further fuel was added to the fire engulfing Elizabeth. Now she wasn't only a bigamist, she was a bigamist who was trying to stifle free speech.

Thousands of people jostled for tickets to the bigamy trial when it opened in April 1776, including the pious Queen Charlotte herself. The general consensus said that Elizabeth was guilty, and speculation over the trial reached a fever pitch. The Duchess of Kingston maintained her dignity in the face of overwhelming evidence, including witnesses who had previously testified that there had been no wedding but were now happy to confirm otherwise. The doctor who delivered Elizabeth's deceased child bore witness against her, and all agreed that she had tricked Kingston into the marriage. There was never any consideration that he might not have been duped at all. Elizabeth was far from blameless, but the duke was no fool either.

Effectively held under house arrest, Elizabeth cut a graceful figure in mourning dress when she attended Westminster Hall with a small number of respectful attendants. Yet, as the case went on, her composure faltered until, as Walpole noted, 'she fell into a great passion of tears, and is, or affects to be, very ill.'[3] What would become of her, asked the excited gossips who gathered in coffeehouses at dawn, before making their way to Westminster Hall for the trial. Would she be transported to the colonies in disgrace? Would the Duchess-Countess add jailbird to her roster of infamy?

Elizabeth had made one inexplicable mistake. In 1759, she had taken the damning decision to register the first marriage in the parish church at Lainston. Her motives for doing so are unclear, but perhaps she feared that Kingston might not marry her, and hoped to have the fallback title of Countess of Bristol should she need it. Regardless of her motive and a personal defence that lasted almost an hour, the eventual and unanimous guilty verdict was a foregone conclusion. Had her ill-fated first marriage not left her with the rank of Countess, Elizabeth would almost certainly have been thrown into prison, but she was spared this indignity. Intriguingly, even as the Meadows family pursued the Earl of Bristol – Augustus Hervey – for the money that they claimed his bigamous wife had kept from them, he declined to sue for divorce. Walpole suspected that this was to avoid poking the hornet's nest of his own far from honourable conduct. He'd had more than enough time to prosecute his wife after her second marriage after all, but had held his tongue.

'The Earl, whom she has made a dowager, talks, and seems to act resolution of being divorced; and the Ecclesiastical Court affects to be ashamed, and thunders against the Duchess,' wrote Walpole as the trial raged across the headlines. 'People cry out that the House of Lords

---

3. Cunningham, Peter (ed.) (1861). *The Letters of Horace Walpole, Earl of Orford, Vol VI*. London: Henry G. Bohn, p.327.

cannot grant a divorce after such symptoms of collusion. I beg their pardons; I do not know what the House of Lords cannot do.[4]

Elizabeth's character was destroyed beyond repair. Only her rank spared her from imprisonment and allowed her to escape to the continent, her fortune intact but her reputation in tatters. It was only a matter of time before the Meadows family launched a suit to have the will overturned and Elizabeth needed to leave England behind forever.

If you expect that Elizabeth lived a quiet life in Europe, you'd be mistaken. Instead, she travelled widely with her new lover, Stefano Zannowich, and always found every door open to the Duchess of Kingston. She died in Paris in 1788, unrepentant to the end.

---

4. Walpole, Horace (1843). *Letters of Horace Walpole, Earl of Orford, to Sir Horace Mann, Vol I*. London: Richard Bentley, p.382.

Wigs at the White Hart

In which the king's brother blots more than his copybook...

> I then prayed for you, my dearest love, kissed your dearest little hair, and lay down and dreamt of you, had you on the dear little couch, ten thousand times in my arms kissing you, and telling you how much I loved and adored you, and you seemed pleased: But alas! when I awoke, found it all delusion; nobody by me, but myself at sea.[1]

A love letter from a sailor to his amour may not seem like the source of a national scandal, but when that sailor is the brother of the monarch and the amour is the wife of a nobleman, a simple romance can become so much more.

King George III and his wife, Charlotte of Mecklenburg-Strelitz, were the very model of a royal family who attempted to lead by example. They were pious to a fault, devoted to one another, and driven by the need to ensure that their household was the one by which all others would be judged. The Duchess-Countess might have flirted shamelessly with George II over her proud and almost bare bosom, but in the court of his young successor, such luxuries were entirely off the menu. In a land that was becoming bawdier and more free-wheeling with every passing day, George III set himself the highest standards possible. No wonder that when he tried to apply those same standards to his siblings, they came up wanting.

---

1. Anonymous (1770). *A Full and Complete History of His R—l H—ss the D— of C—d, and Lady G—r, the Fair Adulteress, Vol I*. London: J. Porter and T. Walker, p.100.

George III had been trained for the monarchy. Serious-minded and old before his time, he was everything his brothers were not. They lived a riotous life, gambling and womanising, as rakish as he was buttoned-up, and it was only a matter of time before it ended in tears. Or a case for criminal conversation, at least.

Henrietta and Richard Grosvenor, later 1st Earl Grosvenor, were a power couple par excellence. Famed for his breathtaking wealth, Lord Grosvenor's property portfolio contained half of Mayfair, London's richest district. He also possessed a voracious sexual appetite that he indulged with the cheapest sex workers he could find. Not for him the finest courtesans and their expensive and practised seduction; instead, he preferred girls who could barely scrape together a living, and he had a thing for blondes. Grosvenor's wife, Henrietta, was as far from his ideal sexual partner as could be.

The pockmarked lord had long battled with venereal diseases that had blighted his health and his looks, until his doctors despairingly decided that the only cure could be a wife. How they thought that might stop a womanising Georgian is anyone's guess, but when he found the beautiful Henrietta Vernon sheltering from a rainstorm in Kensington Gardens, the stage was set for romance. She accepted a lift home in Grosvenor's carriage, dazzled by the interest of the wealthy royal favourite. Henrietta was the daughter of a politician and fourteen years the junior of the worldly Lord Grosvenor. When she complimented the lord on the opulence of his carriage, he told her that it could be her carriage too if she played her cards right. Within the month, she and Grosvenor were married.

It didn't take Henrietta long to realise that she had made a terrible mistake. Her husband continued to visit the brothels and backstreets of London, and when he wasn't doing that, he was gambling away a fortune, even losing more than £250,000 in one memorable night. The young and lively Henrietta wanted some excitement of her own, and she found it in Prince Henry, Duke of Cumberland and Strathearn, brother of King George III. The couple began a passionate affair, but just like Lady Di and Lady Beaufort, Lady Grosvenor was to discover that passionate affairs were not so easy to hide in a house filled with domestic servants.

When Lord Grosvenor found a letter from Cumberland in his wife's bedroom, Henrietta assured him that the duke had merely taken a liking to one of her ladies, and Grosvenor went along with the ruse. Unbeknownst to her though, he asked his household staff to watch his wife and report back to him, with the promise of handsome rewards for those who did. Soon the network of spies extended throughout London and into the surrounding countryside. The net was tightening around the duke and the lady.

The matter came to a head when the lovers arranged a secret tryst at the White Hart in St Alban's. Cumberland was instantly recognisable thanks to his typically Hanoverian features and a startling set of white eyelashes, and he stood out in a crowd. He certainly stood out in St Alban's, where an interested audience listened at the door and peered through a specially drilled hole to spy on the couple's liaison. Someone sent word to Lord Grosvenor that his wife and her lover were in residence and, at 2.00 am, he burst into their bedroom. There he found the bedlinen rumpled and the fully-clothed lovers engaged in nothing more damning than a game of cards. In Georgian London, rumpled bedlinen and a game of cards added up to only one thing: Grosvenor had missed discovering the couple in each other's arms by mere minutes.

When the story of Lady Henrietta and the Duke of Cumberland hit the headlines, the nation lapped it up. The king was apoplectic and so was the philandering baron, who was not about to be made a cuckold. In 1770, Grosvenor petitioned Doctors' Commons, the lower ecclesiastical court, for an annulment.

Yet Grosvenor was no fool and, in his suit, he freely admitted that he had once been a pleasure seeker. Marriage, he lied, had changed him into a loving and faithful husband, who found himself saddled with an immoral and perverted wife. The press wasn't having any of it, and mockingly nicknamed Grosvenor the *Cheshire Cornuto*, or cuckold, reminding everyone that this was no innocent, but a fellow whose sexual appetites were as voracious as they were twisted. Perhaps fearing that the trial might not go all his way, Grosvenor requested an audience with

George III and offered to drop the suit if the king paid him compensation of £100,000, but the monarch sent him packing. If Grosvenor had been banking on George's fear of embarrassment, he was to be disappointed.

The lovers, meanwhile, kept on loving. They enjoyed secret meetings at a milliner's house and began to attend public engagements as a couple, which only stoked Grosvenor's fury. As far as people were concerned, Henrietta's affair was karma and her husband was getting what he deserved. This didn't mean that they were any kinder to Henrietta though. She became the subject of bawdy songs and pamphlets, and as many people believed she was a wicked woman as believed her husband was a profligate waste of space. Nobody could come out of this a winner.

The crim con trial of Grosvenor versus Cumberland began at the Court of King's Bench before Lord Mansfield on 5 July 1770. The main parties were notable by their absence, but one can understand why they chose not to appear since the vast majority of the case was taken up with details of their sex lives. Witness after witness testified against Lady Grosvenor, but most damning of all was the statement of Countess Camilla D'Onhoff. She claimed that the couple had trysted at her home in Cavendish Square, using the excuse that they wished to discuss the naval career of Henrietta's brother privately. The countess, however, testified that she had walked in on the half-naked baroness and the duke in the dining room, having passionate and energetic sex. Cumberland roared at her to get out and close the door, all without missing so much as a stroke. Afterwards, Lady Grosvenor apologised and promised that it would never happen again, but, a few days later, Countess D'Onhoff witnessed an action replay.

The prosecution augmented its case with explicit love letters from the duke, which had been intercepted by the staff at Grosvenor House. Far from titillating, the letters were long-winded, full of misspellings and generally dull. Cumberland was no Romeo. Worse still, witnesses told stories of Cumberland's strange disguises, which employed haystack-like wigs and comedy yokel voices, all of which he hoped would throw suspicious spectators off the scent.

The Duke of Cumberland's legal team was quick to respond, and it presented to the court five young sex workers who were champing at the bit to spill the beans on the lascivious Grosvenor. One of them even claimed that she had passed his coach on the road one day, and had glimpsed Lord and Lady Grosvenor through the window. Upon seeing her, Lord Grosvenor abandoned Lady Henrietta, leapt onto a horse and caught up with his mistress. After a brief sexual encounter, he returned to his wife in the coach as though nothing untoward had happened. Lord Grosvenor even asked Lady Grosvenor if she would give the young lady a job, a request that fell on deaf ears. The defence argued that, far from seeking an annulment from his wife, it was she who should 'be divorced from bed, board and mutual cohabitation with the said Richard lord Grosvenor her husband, by reason of his adultery, committed by him as aforesaid.'[2]

Lord Mansfield told the jury that they must not be swayed by rank and royalty when it came to reaching their verdict. Instead, they should take pains to judge the evidence on its merit. Yet Mansfield was a known royalist sympathiser, and there was no question that Cumberland was guilty of criminal conversation with Lady Grosvenor. Lord Mansfield knew it too; he was simply trying to get as cheap a settlement for the royal household as he could.

Three hours later, the verdict was in: Lady Grosvenor was guilty of adultery, and Cumberland must pay damages of £10,000. Thanks to the indisputable evidence of his own wrongdoing, Grosvenor didn't get his annulment. Instead, he was obliged to pay alimony of £1,200 to his wife for the rest of his days. The Duke of Cumberland couldn't afford to settle the claim for damages and appealed to his brother, George III, to pay the bill on his behalf. When the king refused, it fell to the government to settle Lord Grosvenor's damages from the public purse.

Lady Grosvenor was free of her husband, but the scandal had left her reputation and social cache in tatters. Cast adrift, she found an understanding home as a member of the New Female Coterie, a gathering of women who were considered outsiders from polite society.

---

2. Anonymous (1771). *Copies of the Depositions of the Witnesses Examined in the Cause of Divorce Now Depending in the Consistory Court of the Lord Bishop of London, at Doctor's-Commons*. London: J. Russell, p.306.

Unapologetic and adventurous, these demi-mondaines fascinated the press and public alike with their refusal to toe the accepted line. Lady Grosvenor married for the second time within two months of being widowed in 1802. Her new husband was George Porter, her long-term romantic partner, who was a Whig MP and later became 6th Baron de Hochepied. Lady Grosvenor lived for a further twenty-six happy and contented years. The Duke of Cumberland married commoner Anne Horton in 1771, hot on the heels of the celebrated Grosvenor scandal. The marriage, which was kept secret for some time, caused Cumberland to be banished from the royal court for years.

The Murder of Miss Ray

In which a celebrated diva falls victim to a jealous lover...

When Lord Sandwich was first acquainted with the fatal catastrophe of Miss Ray, he gave it no credit, he however sent a servant to the Shakespeare, with whom a surgeon returned to his Lordship. — When informed that she was really dead, and died in the manner above described, he wrung his hands and cried, exclaiming: — 'I could have borne any thing but this; but this unmans me.'[1]

The tale of Miss Martha Ray is not so much a scandal as a tragedy. It sent a shockwave through the English upper classes, where Martha was a regular fixture of the capital's social scene. Her death was a reminder that life in the glittering heart of London society brought with it not only glamorous rewards but gritty danger too. Gentlemen might fight duels for their honour and that of the women in their lives, but those same women could be at the mercy of much darker forces.

Martha Ray was born in Clerkenwell, the daughter of a corsetmaker and a domestic servant. Her circumstances could not have been more different than those of the man she met when she was just 17 years old, and who remained at her side to the end of her life, nearly 17 years later.

John Montagu, 4th Earl of Sandwich, was nearly three decades Martha Ray's senior and no shrinking violet. He was a devotee of the Hellfire Club, where he could often be glimpsed in the company of his long-time mistress, the celebrated sex worker, Fanny Murray. Fanny had embarked on her illustrious career at the age of 14, and Sandwich had kept a nude portrait of her in his private apartments, which he

---

1. *London Evening Post.* 8 April 1802; issue 8893.

proudly showed off to his male guests. Of course, Sandwich also took a respectable wife, and his marriage to Dorothy, daughter of Viscount Fane, had been rocky long before Martha Ray came onto the scene. Lady Sandwich suffered from mental illness, and Lord Sandwich's open philandering did little to ease her travails. Instead, she fled the family home and took apartments at Windsor Castle. By the time Sandwich met Martha Ray, the couple had been living separate lives for years.

When Martha met Sandwich, the earl was immediately smitten. He was determined to make the teenage apprentice milliner his next mistress and set about shaping her into the woman of his dreams. Sandwich sent the young lady to France, where she was taught the ways of a gentlewoman, and her fine yet untutored voice was honed into a talent worthy of the professional stage. When Martha returned to England, it was as the mistress of Lord Sandwich, but this was no clandestine affair. Instead, Sandwich moved Martha into his home, and the two lived together as husband and wife. Sandwich never made any effort to seek a divorce, and neither did Martha press him to at first. It was simply the way of things in the Georgian era.

Lord Sandwich set Martha up with her own residence and she bore him five children. Yet despite the trappings of wealth that she enjoyed, Martha was ostracised by many of the earl's grandest friends, and her situation was a curiously tricky one. Martha's glamorous life was entirely dependent on staying in Sandwich's favour and, as the years passed, she became ever more aware of the difference in their ages. Should Sandwich die without marrying her, she would be left with nothing, but Martha knew that she had no hope of marriage whilst Lady Dorothy still lived. Even Martha's threats to take up a career on the operatic stage wouldn't move the Earl of Sandwich. He simply wouldn't divorce Lady Dorothy.

In 1775, Lord Sandwich introduced Martha to James Hackman, an army officer. Hackman was dazzled by the celebrated Miss Ray, and when the two became friends, his obsession grew. Though speculation later suggested that the pair had been lovers, no evidence existed to support this assertion. Instead, it simply seemed as though Martha's friendly demeanour towards the young man led him to believe that the two of them might have a future together. It is a familiar and tragic tale even today.

Eventually, Hackman made his move and proposed to Martha. She turned him down, but he pressed his point until she retorted that she would 'never marry a knapsack', a sure sign that what friendship there had been was over. It must have come as a huge relief to Martha when Hackman was posted to Ireland, where she no doubt hoped that he would soon forget his obsession with her.

Instead, Hackman decided that a change of career was in order. He gave up the army and entered the clergy instead, eventually becoming the minister of Wiveton parish in Norfolk. When he proposed for a second time, he was certain that Martha would accept with open arms. What could be a more respectable existence than that of a vicar's wife, after all? Once again, he travelled to the Sandwich home at Hinchingbrooke and, four years after he had proposed for the first time, he repeated his offer. Once again, he was rejected.

We can't be sure whether Martha gave Hackman a second thought once she had sent him on his way, but his every thought was of her and how he might satisfy his obsession. On 7 April 1779, he returned to her home. There he was received by Martha's friend, Caterina Galli, who immediately asked him to leave. Unbeknownst to Martha, when she and Caterina set out for Covent Garden to watch a performance of the comic opera, *Love in a Village*, Hackman followed them. Upon their arrival at the opera house, he observed the two women meeting William Hanger, 3rd Baron Coleraine, and became convinced that the baron was his rival for Martha's affections.

As Martha and Caterina went into the theatre, Hackman returned home and penned two letters. One was a suicide note addressed to his brother, the other an obsessive love letter to Martha Ray. In its pages, he expressed 'a profession of the warmest expressions of love and tenderness; hopes he will be soon settled in a situation capable of making them both happy for life, and declaring that no good, no happiness can he enjoy, not even life can he sustain without her.'[2] Then Hackman loaded two

---

2. *General Advertiser and Morning Intelligencer.* 9 April 1779; issue 657.

pistols and set out into the night to observe the comings and goings at the theatre. Consumed with jealous rage, Hackman intended to kill Martha Ray and turn the second weapon on himself.

Martha and Caterina exited the opera house into the hustle and bustle of Covent Garden, but were unable to reach their coach through the milling audience members. Seeing their plight, an attorney named John McNamara came to their aid and cleared a path for the women through the crowd. Unseen by him, a black-clad figure followed the trio towards the waiting carriage and, as McNamara helped Caterina Galli into the vehicle, the man in black made his move. Fruit seller Mary Anderson witnessed the horrifying scene, and later told all during a sensational trial at the Old Bailey:

> I was standing at the post. Just as the play broke up I saw two ladies and a gentleman coming out of the playhouse; a gentleman in black followed them. Lady Sandwich's coach was called. When the carriage came up, the gentleman handed the other lady into the carriage; the lady that was shot stood behind. Before the gentleman could come back to hand her into the carriage the gentleman in black came up, laid hold of her by the gown, and pulled out of his pocket two pistols; he shot the right hand pistol at her, and the other at himself. She fell with her hand so (describing it as being on her forehead) and died before she could be got to the first lamp; I believe she died immediately, for her head hung directly. At first I was frightened at the report of the pistol, and ran away. He fired another pistol, and dropped immediately. They fell feet to feet. He beat himself violently over the head with his pistols, and desired somebody would kill him.[3]

Hackman's planned suicide had failed. Instead, he was apprehended, drenched in Martha's blood and bleeding badly from the beating he had given himself. Yet, as he was taken into custody, he declared that Martha

---

3. Old Bailey Proceedings Online (www.oldbaileyonline.org, version 8.0, 11 August 2021), April 1779, trial of JAMES HACKMAN (t17790404-3).

Ray had been the author of her own misfortune. 'What a change has a few hours made in me,' lamented the murderer. 'Had her friends done as I wished them to do, this would never have happened.[4]

When Martha's body was examined at the nearby Shakespeare Tavern, it was observed that the single shot had been immediately fatal. The ball had penetrated her forehead and exited her skull near her left ear. The coroner's inquest made a finding of wilful murder. The murder-suicide, intended to be the final expression of Hackman's deadly fixation, had left Martha Ray dead. Her killer, far from dying at her side, would stand trial at the Old Bailey.

Lord Sandwich was bereft when news of the attack reached him and immediately sent a surgeon to Martha's side in the hope that she might be saved. When his agent confirmed the awful news, he was shattered. The rake who had once partied at the Hellfire Club locked the doors of his private chambers and wept. His spirits never truly recovered from the loss of the woman he had adored.

The stories of Martha Ray and James Hackman, the man who had stalked and murdered her, were inextricably bound together and, before the night was out, the scandalous case became the talk of the town. As Hackman's trial gripped the nation, the horrific story of obsessive murder was reinterpreted by some as a romantic tragedy, and Martha's death as the price one paid for sin. It was a crime of passion, said the prevailing opinion, and Hackman was to be pitied as much as blamed. Martha had rejected Hackman time and again, yet some correspondents sought to blame her for her own murder; sadly, it is a pattern we still see today.

Hackman played up this version of events, claiming that he had meant Martha no harm, but had only intended to kill himself in front of her. Seeing Martha on the arm of another man had driven him to murder, he said, and he produced the letter he had written to his brother as proof of his initial plans. Yet this made no sense when one considered the two pistols or the letter he had written to Martha, and the Old Bailey showed no mercy. James Hackman was sentenced to death.

---

4. *London Evening Post*. 8–10 April 1779; issue 8893.

An immense crowd gathered to watch James Hackman hang at Tyburn, but the behaviour of the executioner lent further weight to the fact that Hackman was seen as the victim, rather than the perpetrator. Hackman's hands were bound only gently, and his request for a period of private prayer once the noose was around his neck was granted without question. He prayed for 10 minutes, then dropped his handkerchief to signal that he was ready. As James Hackman hanged, the weeping crowd recited prayers for his soul.

The last word in this tale shouldn't belong with James Hackman, but to Martha Ray. She was laid to rest in a vault beneath St Nicholas' Church, Elstree, until renovations were undertaken in 1824. At that time, Martha's remains were reburied in the churchyard, but no marker stood over her grave. In 1920 the incumbent Earl of Sandwich erected a tombstone where she lay, and Martha Ray was celebrated once more.

The Heroine of St Ann's Hill

In which a celebrated courtesan risks everything for love…

> For some days past it has been confidently reported, that the Hon.
> Charles Fox had rewarded the constancy and other merits of Mrs
> Armstead [*sic*] with his hand at the altar. We since learn, that on
> landing on the Continent, she was presented as Mrs Fox. The wit
> and accomplishments of this Lady have long been justly celebrated,
> and she is as much entitled to every privilege that the event we
> allude to can confer upon her, as many Ladies who preside over
> fashion in the present laxity of her manners.[1]

Fiction is replete with tales of professional courtesans who give up their
careers for love. Some end happily, a lot end badly, and all of them are the
heroines of their own romantic sagas, bruised on the battlefield of their
profession and determined not to fall in love. Until they do. Elizabeth
Armistead might have been the blueprint for all of them, and her story
encompasses a notorious prince, plenty of rich men and even a career as
a political hostess. Her rise from mysterious origins to the pinnacle of
respectability might not be that of the typical courtesan of fiction, but it
was certainly not uncommon in the Georgian world.

Where Elizabeth Bridget Armistead, née Cane, came from is a matter
of conjecture. Of Elizabeth's parents we know nothing, and though
rumours of preachers, cobblers and market men were scattered here and
there, her origins remain a mystery. Perhaps she had been a servant or a
hairdresser's assistant, perhaps she hadn't; perhaps she had worked in the
theatre, perhaps not. Other than confirming that she had been born in

---

1. *Aberdeen Journal*. 18 August 1802; issue 2849.

1750, Elizabeth kept the details of her early life deliberately mysterious. As a result, she seemed to have come from nowhere, emerging fully formed and perfectly skilled into the pleasure-filled world of Georgian London as *Mrs Armistead*. And the clients who flocked to the brothel where she worked couldn't get enough of her.

There appeared to be no Mr Armistead or, if there was, he was long since departed by the time Liz came to the public eye. The very first evidence of her existence came courtesy of the great Sir Joshua Reynolds, whose appointment book listed a sitting with Mrs Armistead at Mrs Mitchell's, an upmarket Soho brothel on Upper St John Street.

Like all enterprising courtesans, Liz was determined to land herself a wealthy patron who would take her out of the brothel and give her the existence of a lady, making her mistress to one instead of many. She hit the big time when she charmed a succession of titled men, capping them with the notorious Bully, 2nd Viscount Bolingbroke, who you may recall broke Lady Diana Spencer's heart. Famed for his glittering, profligate life, Bully was nothing but a stepping stone for Mrs Armistead, and he opened the door for her next expected triumph: a glittering career on the stage.

So far, life seemed to just fall into place for Liz. Little wonder that when she strolled out onto the stage of the Covent Garden Playhouse in 1774, she expected a standing ovation. Instead, she got the sort of notices that might break a lesser performer.

Liz, of course, knew that no publicity was bad publicity, especially when a girl had a rich patron to bankroll her. Bully had done his bit and she moved on to settle in an opulent Bond Street property paid for by General Richard Smith, a leading light in the East India Company. Here she lived a life of leisure, indulging herself with the occasional acting role in and around appointments with her many, ever-grander patrons.

General Smith was supplanted by John Frederick Sackville, 3rd Duke of Dorset, who crops up more than once in these pages, but their relationship wasn't to last. Dorset jettisoned her for a scandalous liaison with the Countess of Derby, even as Liz added Lady Derby's husband to her list of clients. Never let it be said that the love life of Georgian high society wasn't tangled.

Yet for Liz, these rich patrons were nothing but a means to an end. Their money financed her lifestyle and allowed her to indulge her true passion: politics. Many of her patrons were influential Whigs, and Elizabeth opened her house to party supporters as both a meeting place and a political salon. It was this that brought her into the same circle as the famed Whig statesman, Charles James Fox. He and Liz had met once before when he pranked Bully by kicking down the bedroom door while the couple were busy inside.

Though Fox and Liz soon developed an abiding friendship, there was no hint of romance just yet. Besides, Liz had just reached the peak of her career: she had snared the interest of George, the rakish and profligate Prince of Wales. He also happened to be one of Fox's best friends.

In Mrs Armistead, the Prince of Wales had more than met his match. She didn't capitulate straight away, but made him work to get her interest. Yet being squired by the Prince of Wales, who brought with him influence, glamour and invitations, had its downside too. George's Tory opponents decried Liz as a honeytrap, who was employing her sexual wiles to snare the prince in Whig intrigues, but the truth was more prosaic than that. George was perfectly happy to be ensnared by any attractive woman, regardless of her politics. Far from a scheming political tool in the hands of the opposition, Elizabeth was living life on her own terms and the Prince of Wales didn't hold any lasting fascination for her. When his appeal and allowance wore thin, Liz took a European trip with another gentleman, leaving her royal paramour to drown his sorrows. As we'll learn elsewhere, he did it in fine style and remained good friends with Mrs Armistead to the end of his days.

When Liz returned to England, it was to a new life with Charles Fox. Always a regular caller to her Surrey home at St Ann's Hill, he now took a step beyond friendship and became not only her patron, but her lover. The courtesan who had once held all of London in the palm of her hand had, quite unexpectedly, fallen in love with the man who had been her friend for years. The relationship took everyone by surprise, but it was a true love and intellectual match, and Liz gave up her career and her coterie of rich supporters to become a one-man woman. Yet no patrons meant no money and Fox, himself a profligate gambler, was in no position to help her. Rather than betray Fox with the wealthy men who would happily help her out of her financial difficulties, Liz sold off her belongings one by one, learning for the first time how to balance a budget.

Yet Liz wasn't the only one who turned her back on offers of cash. When Fox was offered the opportunity to marry into serious money, she volunteered to step aside to let him do so, but he refused to even consider it. There was only one woman for Fox, and he and Liz were married in 1795. Fearing that marriage to a retired courtesan would damage her husband's political career, Elizabeth begged Fox to keep their union secret. For seven years, nobody was any the wiser.

The truth of the marriage came to light in 1802 when Napoleon invited Fox to France. He insisted on taking his wife with him and, though London society was whipped into a frenzy by the nerve of the pair, the cool Liz negotiated this new territory with grace and dignity. She had known plenty of scandal in her time after all, so this was nothing to be afraid of. There was little mud that could be thrown at such a devoted couple and the Foxes were gradually accepted into society as husband and wife.

Tragically, the Foxes' happiness was to be all too short-lived. Charles Fox died in 1806, and his dying words were for his wife. As he took his last breath, he murmured, 'dearest Liz.'

Heartbroken, Liz went into mourning for the man she had adored. In recognition of his affection for the couple, the Prince of Wales topped up her widow's pension of £1,200 per year by £500. Many of Mrs Armistead's former patrons followed suit, making yearly donations to Liz in recognition of the happy times they had once shared.

As she grew older, Liz's scandalous past was gradually overtaken by her new life of respectable philanthropy. The woman who had once been a notorious symbol of opulence became an elder stateswoman of the Whigs, commanding respect and affection in equal measure. She lived to the grand old age of 92, having spanned the Georgian era, the Regency and the dawn of the Victorian age.

When Liz was laid to rest at All Saints in Chertsey, the little church was crowded not only by her friends but by those who had known her by reputation alone. They were united by the simple need to pay their respects to the woman whose kindness, charity and grace had endeared her to people from all classes and all walks of life.

A Whisper of Scandal: The Spectral Stalker

Henrietta Ponsonby, Countess of Bessborough, was the sister of Georgiana, Duchess of Devonshire, and the mother of Lady Caroline Lamb. She more than matched both for scandal. Henrietta had enough lovers to fill a book, and so enchanted Richard Brinsley Sheridan that he promised to return and haunt her after his death.

The Ladies of Llangollen

In which the 'two most celebrated virgins in Europe' build a remarkable home, in more ways than one.

> Lady Eleanor Butler and Miss Ponsonby were Irish young ladies of rank and beauty, who loved each other with an affection so true that they could never bear the idea of the separation which the marriage of either would necessitate. They, therefore, resolved on lives of celibacy, and, refusing many handsome offers, fled from home. … It is said that, although Lady Eleanor arrived here in the natural aspect of a pretty girl, Miss Ponsonby accompanied her in the guise of smart footman, in top boots and buskin breeches.[1]

There is an oft-repeated myth that Queen Victoria did not believe that lesbians existed, because she couldn't imagine that there was anything they could *do* together. Like most of the best stories of clueless monarchs, it isn't true, but the tale of the ladies of Llangollen is filled with commentators that were keen to assume they were two heterosexual women who practised celibacy because their platonic bond was too strong to let a man come between them. It's not unusual to see efforts to explain away same-sex relationships between women as intense friendships. Whereas Georgian law treated sexual intercourse between men as a capital crime that could be punishable by death, the love between women was more often dismissed as nothing more than platonic intimacy. Sometimes that might have been the case, but for the ladies of Llangollen, it seems unlikely.

---

1. Pritchard, J. (1895). *An Account of the Ladies of Llangollen*. Llangollen: H. Jones, p.1.

Sarah Ponsonby and Lady Eleanor Butler were the very best of friends, despite the sixteen-year age gap that lay between them. They had both been born to notable families, and Lady Eleanor could boast the Earl – later Dukes – of Ormond among her people. Following their initial meeting in 1768, when Sarah was just 13, they quickly became close friends. As the years passed and their connection deepened, the two women longed to escape the conventions of society and live a life of their own making.

A decade after that first meeting, Sarah disguised herself in men's clothes, scooped up her little dog, and hurried in the dead of night to a barn where Lady Eleanor awaited. Together they fled for the coast, where they hoped to board a boat to England and a life of joyful seclusion.

Fate had other ideas. Alerted by the barking of Sarah's dog, their respective families gave chase and the women were forced to return to their homes, but this was merely the beginning of their story. As the months passed, Sarah and Lady Eleanor refused to think or speak of anything but each other. If they were not allowed to leave with the blessing of their families, they declared, then they would abscond again and again, as many times as they had to. The only comfort their relatives could take from all of this was the knowledge that 'there was no man concerned with either of them.'[2] As far as their families were willing to admit, they were simply eccentric friends, and that was far preferable to a ruined daughter.

Faced with the certain knowledge that the women's minds would not be changed, the Ponsonby and Butler families eventually acquiesced to Sarah and Lady Eleanor's wishes to leave Ireland. Though their families eventually thawed, at first the women were ostracised and left to fend for themselves. And they couldn't have been happier. They toured Wales and settled in Llangollen with Sarah's loyal maid, Mary Caryll, who would serve them faithfully to the end of her days. Later, when all three women were dead, they were buried together in the same shared plot.

Though their first home in Wales was rented, in 1780 the two women purchased a cottage that they named Plas Newydd, or New Mansion.

---

2. Bell, Eva Mary (ed.) (1930). *The Hamwood Papers of the Ladies of Llangollen and Caroline Hamilton*. London: Macmillan and Company, p.30.

1. A Scene from *The Beggar's Opera*. By William Hogarth, 1729. (Lavinia Fenton kneels on the right. Her future husband, the Duke of Bolton, watches from the far right.)

2. Miss Kitty Fisher as *Cleopatra Dissolving the Pearl*. By Edward Fisher, after Sir Joshua Reynolds, c.1752–1763.

3. Maria, Countess of Coventry. By Gavin Hamilton, 1753.

4. Mrs Horton, later Viscountess Maynard. By Sir Joshua Reynolds, c.1767–69.

5. *The Third Duke of Grafton Divorcing His First Wife*. By Anonymous, 1769.

6. Lady Elizabeth Stanley, Countess of Derby. By Sir George Romney, 1776–78.

7. Elizabeth Chudleigh, the Duchess of Kingston. By Anonymous (undated).

8. The Ladies of Llangollen. By J.H. Lynch, after Mary Parker, 1828.

FLORIZEL AND PERDITA.

9. *Florizel and Perdita.*
By Anonymous, 1783.
(George IV and Mary
Robinson are shown as
one person.)

10. William Beckford.
By Francesco Bartolozzi,
1772.

11. Emma, Lady Hamilton.
By John Jones, after Sir George
Romney, 1785.

12. *The Disconsolate Sailor.* By Charles Williams Argus, 1811. (Catherine Tylney-Long chooses William Wellesley-Pole over the Duke of Clarence.)

13. *Lady Caroline Lamb in Her Page's Dress.* By Anonymous (undated).

Lord Biron

14. Memorial Portrait of Lord Byron. By Mathieu Barathier, 1826.

15. Marguerite, Countess of Blessington. By Sir Thomas Lawrence, 1822.

16. *The Rat Catcher.* By Henry Heath, 1825. (The Duke of Wellington and Harriette Wilson discuss her memoirs.)

Here they could finally live as they wished, and they did it in style. Plas Newydd was a simple five-room home when they moved in, but over the years the ladies expanded the house considerably, decorating it in an eccentric Gothic manner with a patchwork of reclaimed oak panelling and stained glass. Their gardens flourished and the house morphed into the sanctuary they had always dreamed of. But paradise came at a price, and the couple were never far from debt. Gossip soon spread about the unusual ladies who lived such a secluded existence, but all they wanted was to be left alone. There was no scandal here, just three people living a happy life together.

The ladies of Llangollen were a local curiosity, but soon they unwittingly became so much more than that. As word spread of the house and its inhabitants, the most famous figures in the country wanted to see Plas Newydd for themselves. A glance at the names of their visitors reads like a *Who's Who* of Georgian society. Literary legends such as Byron, Shelley and Wordsworth beat a path to that celebrated door in Wales, whilst Sarah's distant and scandalous relative Lady Caroline Lamb paid a call, and Wellington was always assured of a warm welcome. Visitors travelled from Europe just to catch a glimpse of the fascinating ladies and Queen Charlotte longed to see their cottage, eventually persuading King George III to pay them a pension in recognition of their unspoiled, unassuming existence.

Yet despite their fame, in their day-to-day habits, the ladies themselves lived simple lives. They dressed in a manner that was thought of as eccentric, favouring riding habits and top hats, as well as short hair and powder. Their appearance was derided as outdated and masculine, but the women's supporters argued that this was merely sensible garb for people who lived an outdoor lifestyle, where silk and lace wouldn't last five minutes. Though they were extravagant when it came to decorating their home, the women were far from flamboyant and adhered to what they proudly referred to as 'our System'. They studied, they read, and they remained secluded in their ever-growing house, doing everything to the same, strict schedule, and keeping exhaustive journals of their activities. It was, as Patricia Hampl notes in her study of the ladies, a monastic way of life.

There is nothing in the writings of Ponsonby and Butler that indicates the ladies lived a life of particular sexual excitement. When a report in the *General Evening Post* of July 1791 suggested that they were lesbians, the women considered a lawsuit. We ask ourselves, then, if this means that they really were merely friends, but I think not. Rather, theirs was a life of absolute and shared contentment. Each had found in the other their perfect opposite, the mirror of their self, a love for the ages, and it was a love that they were prepared to fiercely protect. To see it splashed across the press was abhorrent to them.

In a world that was changing, the ladies of Llangollen remained perfectly peaceful in their sanctuary. The eighteenth century slipped into the nineteenth, monarchs came and went, celebrity visitors kept calling, and still Sarah and Lady Eleanor remained unchanged, tending their house and garden, writing their precise journals of days well spent, and reading. Always reading.

Slowly, though, time began to encroach on their idyllic existence. Mary Caryll, their faithful maid, died in 1809. The elder of the ladies of Llangollen, Lady Eleanor Butler, passed away at the grand old age of 90 in 1829, followed two years later by Sarah Ponsonby. From that first ill-fated attempt at elopement, they had achieved the seemingly impossible. They had lived by their own rules, at a time when so many women were unable to do so. Some thought them eccentric, others thought them visionaries, but the ladies of Llangollen didn't take much interest in what other people called them. They answered to nobody but themselves.

A Whisper of Scandal: Playing Both Sides

Guiseppina Grassini never liked to take sides. This celebrated opera diva became Napoleon's lover after his decisive victory at Marengo, but eventually left him for quick-fingered violinist Pierre Rode. As Napoleon languished in exile years later, Guiseppina found a new lover in the shape of the Duke of Wellington, the very man who had vanquished her former beau!

A Family Affair

In which half-siblings carry on a family tradition of scandal...

Lord BOLINGBROKE is an enthusiastic admirer of *Shakespeare*,
and, among many others, often quotes this passage in *Lear.* — 'To
both these SISTERS I have sworn my *love!*'[1]

Lady Diana Spencer and her husband, the appropriately-nicknamed
Bully, had given polite society enough gossip to last a lifetime, but the
House of Bolingbroke was far from done with the headlines. Lady Di's
marriage to Bully, aka 2nd Viscount Bolingbroke, ended in a messy
divorce, and their children did little to set the family name back on a
respectable footing.

George Richard St John, the eldest son of Bully and Lady Di,
inherited the title of Viscount Bolingbroke on his father's death in 1787.
By that time, he had already served a term in Parliament, entering the
Commons at the age of 21 and remaining there until 1784.

It was during Bolingbroke's short parliamentary career that he married
Charlotte Collins, the daughter of his boyhood tutor. Whilst he was
busy fathering three children, however, the woman who would be the
other leading player in our story was living a rather more sheltered life.

Mary Beauclerk was the daughter of Lady Di and her second husband,
Topham Beauclerk. You may recall that Lady Di's affair with Beauclerk
had been the catalyst that ended her unhappy marriage, and Mary was
one of a pair of twins who were born to Lady Di and her lover during
their affair. Mary's sister, Elizabeth, married her first cousin, George

---

1. *The Times.* 7 July 1789; issue 1199.

Herbert, 11th Earl of Pembroke, but Elizabeth's love affair was to be much closer to home than that.

Just as his father had been a gambler with a love of wild living, so too was the heir. George St John borrowed money extravagantly and lost it just as easily, and he made for heady company indeed. In early 1787, shortly before Bully died, George and Charlotte St John hosted a visit from George's half-sister Mary Beauclerk. During this fateful visit, the half-siblings crossed the line of friendship and began a sexual relationship. Mary fell pregnant almost immediately, and their next steps almost beggar belief.

Rather than try to conceal their relationship from Charlotte, who had borne her husband three children in less than five years, they regaled her with the details. Charlotte took the news in a surprisingly sanguine manner, perhaps out of some misguided sense of loyalty to her husband, perhaps because she had only just gained the title of Viscountess Bolingbroke on the death of her father-in-law. Perhaps she was even suffering from a surfeit of compassion for her spouse, whose childhood travails would be well known to her. He was the child of divorced parents, isolated from the scandalous mother who had left her children to pursue her own happiness, and raised by a father whose excesses fuelled the gossip columns for years. Maybe Charlotte simply feared the same public humiliation that her mother-in-law had suffered. Whatever the reason, she stood by her man. She took Mary to France and there the baby was born. On their return to England, the infant was slipped quietly into the Bolingbroke nursery.

Yet, Charlotte's understanding did little to teach Mary and George a lesson and, a little over a year later, the women were travelling back to France. Once again, they returned to England with another baby to add to the Bolingbroke nursery, and nobody suspected that anything was amiss at all. It was a wide-eyed, infinitely eligible Mary Beauclerk who was back in London for the season, charming all who knew her with her innocent manner and unassuming ways. Behind the scenes though, the lovers were plotting. There was a limit to the number of babies Charlotte could bring home from France before the gossips put two and two together and realised the sheer magnitude of the scandal that had occurred right under their noses. Bolingbroke and Mary intended to beat them to it. They eloped to France together with their little family, leaving Lady Bolingbroke and her children to pick up the pieces in England.

In June 1789, the Barton family left England for Paris. What made the Barton family unique was that it didn't exist at all. Instead, it was the travelling name adopted by Viscount Bolingbroke, a pregnant Mary Beauclerk and their two children. There would be no going back for the couple now, and no chance of keeping their relationship secret any longer. Equally, there would be few, if any, people willing to fight the corner of a couple of incestuous lovers. Their transgression was beyond the pale and it goes without saying that it was illegal. This was not the kind of scandal that would simply blow over and be forgotten, or be allowed to settle down into some sort of grudging respectability. They had crossed the Rubicon.

Paris was a city on the edge of revolution, but in its teeming streets the Barton family hoped to pass unnoticed. From their lodgings, Mary wrote to Lady Di, not only *her* mother, but the mother of her lover too. She admitted that they were in love and intended to live forever on the continent under an assumed name. Lady Di, who had maintained her privacy since her own headline-grabbing divorce, fell into such despair at the shocking news that for a time there were fears for her life. The cat was completely out of the bag and, in the drawing rooms of society, there was no greater topic of conversation than Mary and Bolingbroke's affair.

The deteriorating political situation in France made it a bad bet for a new start, and the couple fled the chaotic city for the more settled environs of Germany. Here they made a home, but Viscount Bolingbroke began to tire of Mary just as he had tired of the wife who had been so accommodating to his sister-mistress and their offspring. Mary gave birth to two more children by Bolingbroke, but the thrill of the affair was gone. What had once upon a time been exciting, transgressive and forbidden now became commonplace. Mary no longer held any mystery for Viscount Bolingbroke.

Bolingbroke had broken his wife's heart, and now he broke Mary Beauclerk's too. He abandoned her and his four son-nephews to elope with 17-year-old Isabella, Baroness von Hompesch. The couple made for Austria, where they were married. For Bolingbroke, this was a bigamous union, but he somehow managed to convince Isabella that it was legitimate.

In England, the fallout from the scandal continued to blight the life of the family the viscount had left behind. Tired of being the object of sympathy and gossip, Viscountess Bolingbroke travelled with her children to Italy, where she hoped to live in seclusion. Instead, she became the target of the prying eyes of wealthy Britons who visited on their Grand Tour. Eventually, they forced her to return to England and what she hoped would finally be a quiet life.

Perhaps surprisingly, Mary Beauclerk remained in Germany after her abandonment. Bolingbroke had at least agreed to a financial settlement that would make her independent, and since the shocking tale of upper-class incest would follow her wherever she went, there was little point in returning to London if she hoped for a new start. She eventually married Count Franz Jenison von Walworth in 1796 and visited England on honeymoon, a respectable spouse at last. That marriage would eventually produce six children.

When Charlotte, Lady Bolingbroke, died in 1803, her errant husband could legally marry Isabella von Hompesch. Having already fathered seven children with his first wife and his half-sister, he fathered a further four with the new Viscountess Bolingbroke too. Needless to say, none of them was as scandalous as their father. Who could be, after all?

A Whisper of Scandal: See You in Court

Lady Frances Webster enjoyed flirtations with a veritable *Who's Who* of Regency celebrities, but it was her assignation with Wellington that threatened scandal. Upon learning of their affair, Lady Frances's husband, Sir James Webster-Wedderburn, threatened to sue Wellington for an eye-watering £50,000, but his rival somehow persuaded him that there was no truth to the rumours. Instead, Sir James sued a newspaper that had printed allegations of adultery and walked away with a relatively trifling £2,000.

The Lady and the Laudanum

In which rumours of kidnapping are overstated…

> A gentleman and his wife are on a visit; and the gentleman, who used to go to bed after his wife, goes to bed at ten or eleven o'clock, and leaves her up with another man. What must this husband be made of? We must consider him made like no other man … I must consider this husband as giving his wife up to the adulterer. I must look upon him as the negligent author of all the misery that has arisen in consequence of it.[1]

Susanna Harriot Hope appeared to be the perfect model of a respectable wife. Born to a Derbyshire rector and his wife in 1768, by the time she was in her teens she had already been the subject of a portrait by Joseph Wright of Derby, a family friend. At the age of just 17, she married Joseph Biscoe, a nephew of the Duke of Somerset. Biscoe's father had made his fortune as one-half of a wealthy mercantile company named Hilton and Biscoe.

Biscoe and Susanna were married in 1786, and they seemed set for the sort of happy marriage that rarely troubles the pages of this volume. The couple welcomed their first and only child the year after their wedding, and for seven years all was well. They lived in Mansfield and Derbyshire for a time until Biscoe's business interests in the south forced a relocation. This was to be a fateful moment in the marriage of Susanna and Joseph.

During Biscoe's schooldays at Harrow, he had befriended a fellow pupil named Richard Lee. Lee's father, Robert Cooper Lee, was also

---

1. Anonymous (1794). *The Trial of Mrs Biscoe, for Adultery with Robert Gordon, Esq.* London: Allen and West, pp.44–45.

guardian to a younger boy named Robert Home Gordon, who had been born in Jamaica to the immensely wealthy owners of a sugar plantation. Though Gordon studied at Harrow alongside Lee and Biscoe, when he grew up, education was the last thing on his mind. Instead, the dashing and rich young man became a popular figure about town, seen in all the best places and with the most illustrious company.

When Richard Lee heard that Biscoe was looking for a house to rent in the south of England, he recommended that his friend speak to their old school chum, Robert Home Gordon. Gordon was seeking a tenant for his property, Shoreham House, and Biscoe seemed to fit the bill. The let was agreed and Biscoe, Susanna and their daughter, Mary, moved to Shoreham. Shy and unassuming, Biscoe was as different as could be from his new landlord, but the two soon became firm friends.

Gordon, Lee and Biscoe all shared a passion for hunting, and Lee and Gordon often came to stay at Shoreham so the three men could hunt together. Lee's visits were fleeting, but those of Robert Gordon began to grow more protracted until he was spending weeks at a time with Joseph and Susanna. Rather than join his host on long hunts, Gordon began to find excuses to remain at Shoreham with Susanna. On other occasions, the Biscoes went to stay at Gordon's shooting box and appeared to be one big, happy family. Biscoe little suspected it, but his wife and friend were in the midst of a passionate affair.

As we have already seen, whilst it might have been easy to keep husbands in the dark, servants were a different matter. The domestic staff at Shoreham were well aware that something was afoot, and their suspicions were further aroused by the number of times Susanna and Robert had them care for little Mary. Once the child was safely passed to servants, the couple would close the door and enjoy a little alone time. Mere minutes before her husband was due home, Gordon would take his leave and head out as though he had been all day on a shoot, with no mention made of the hours he had spent with Mrs Biscoe. When an exhausted Biscoe returned from his day in the saddle, he would inevitably go to bed early and leave Susanna and Gordon alone once more. What they got up to in those stolen hours hardly needs to be described.

On 21 October 1794, the affair began to unravel. With her husband in London on business, Susanna took a ride in the company of her coachman, Francis Swindel. To Swindel's surprise – not to mention suspicion – the route she chose just happened to result in an unconvincingly impromptu meeting with Gordon. Susanna made sure that the coachman couldn't hear her conversation, but she had underestimated how much she and Gordon had already been observed. That same morning, Susanna's maid, Margaret Sparks, became suspicious that something was afoot when Susanna had attempted to pack some travelling items without her noticing. Someone, and we can't know who, summoned Susanna's two brothers and, by the time she returned from her assignation with Gordon, they were waiting. After a short interview, first with Susanna, then with Gordon, the brothers left the house. Presumably, they had been satisfied by whatever explanation they had been given.

Yet that visit by Susanna's brothers marked the beginning of the end. As soon as the men departed, the servants heard a commotion breaking out in the drawing room where Susanna and Gordon were alone. After a while, Gordon called Susanna's maid into the room and demanded she bring him a bottle of laudanum. Susanna was proclaiming hysterically that she couldn't leave her child and Gordon was agitated, stalking this way and that, fizzing with nervous energy. With no laudanum available, the servants retreated, but sniffing a drama in the offing, housekeeper Mary Feasant hurried out into the garden and watched the unfolding scene through a window.

Feasant reported that Susanna was in deep distress at the prospect of abandoning her daughter at Shoreham. Gordon's furious reply was to tell her that she was not a woman of her word, at which she downed a glass of wine, presumably to calm her nerves. Fearing that Gordon's search for laudanum suggested that he intended to drug and abduct her mistress, Feasant hurried off to tell the coachman what was happening in the drawing room. She returned to find the couple gone, and the better part of two decanters of wine empty.

Susanna Biscoe and Robert Home Gordon had fled into the night. They went on foot, and though Biscoe's coachman gave chase, he wasn't able to catch the couple before they made it to a local inn and procured a carriage. From there they fled for Gordon's home in London's Albemarle Street. Only then did the coachman intercept the couple on the road, but the delay merely caused them to spend a night in an inn before they hastened to London, and into infamy.

What happened next would soon become the subject of a celebrated trial that raised an important question. Could a husband be said to have contributed to his own abandonment and, if so, what penalty should he face when it came to the inevitable lawsuit and claim for damages?

Perhaps surprisingly, Biscoe didn't seek a divorce but instead sued Gordon for criminal conversation and damages of £10,000. The trial opened on 8 December 1794, with Biscoe represented by William Garrow, later Attorney General. Opposite Garrow, Gordon employed the legal nous of Thomas Erskine, a future Lord High Chancellor. All this time, Mrs Biscoe was still living under Mr Gordon's roof and her husband, the timid and unassuming Joseph, was feeling the sting of being the leading man in one of the biggest and most gossiped about trials that London had known for months.

From the start, Gordon and Susanna had no legal leg to stand on. That she was living with Gordon and that he must pay damages for stealing her away was obvious, but what remained to be discussed was exactly *how* she came to be living with her husband's good friend. Joseph Biscoe had no wish to add to his wife's infamy, so his legal team attempted to paint her as a victim of the dissembling, wicked Gordon. They called on household servants to testify, and their suggestions that Gordon had intended to drug his lover with laudanum and carry her away rocked the court. That Susanna had been seen in tears added further fuel to the fire, as did the fact that the couple had slept in different beds during their night at the inn, although they appeared to have spent time in the same bed too. The prosecution maintained that Susanna was an innocent who shouldn't be blamed for her actions, nor for the way that 'Mr. Gordon, openly and in triumph, carried [her] to his house, where she has lived from that time to the present.'[2]

---

2. Ibid., p.9.

At Albemarle Street, the couple lived together openly, though they kept adjoining rooms for the sake of preserving an illusion of decency. At the trial, however, Biscoe's team was able to produce maids who were happy to testify that *criminal conversation* had taken place in the London house. The rakish Gordon had worked a wicked charm over what had once been a happy home, they claimed, bewitching the trusting Susanna and stealing her from under her husband's gentlemanly nose. If they were to be believed, then Gordon must be held wholly responsible.

As one might expect, Gordon's legal representatives had prepared a robust defence. Central to it was the argument that, far from a blissful union, the Biscoe marriage was actually the opposite. This was no dutiful and devoted husband, Erskine posited, but a man who would happily abandon his young and loving wife in favour of the hunt, then retire to bed alone. Was it any surprise, therefore, that Susanna sought romance with Robert Home Gordon, the only man who was gentlemanly enough to give her the attention she craved? By painting their man as the only glimmer of light in a dull life, Gordon's team hoped to mitigate the circumstances of the affair and, crucially, cut down the damages to something less eye-watering than the requested £10,000. There was no point arguing that adultery had not taken place, but pleading mitigating circumstances might still work wonders.

Erskine's rebuttal of the case took no prisoners; he asked exactly what sort of husband would leave his wife with another man during the day, let alone go to bed in the knowledge that said wife and other man were ungoverned and alone together into the early hours. Even worse was the evidence given by a deeply reluctant Richard Lee, the man who had brought Gordon and Biscoe back into each other's lives. He admitted that he had first raised the issue of Susanna and Gordon's close relationship with Biscoe in the summer. Lee had suggested that they always go out as a foursome and that Susanna and Gordon not be allowed to ride together. Biscoe dismissed the suggestion, telling him, 'Let them go on by themselves, they are made for one another.' When asked why he didn't intervene, Lee said that it wasn't his place. If the husband didn't care enough, then why would he insinuate himself into another man's marriage? This was the moment for Biscoe to act and end the intrigue before it was out of control, Erskine argued. If he had failed to do so, then he alone bore the responsibility for the sorry situation that followed.

In summing up, Lord Chief Justice Kenyon asked the jury to consider all that they had heard before they reached their verdict. There was much to weigh up:

> On the part of the Defendant they tell you, that Mr Biscoe has stood by and seen his wife debauched; and, if that is so, he is one of the most atrocious men living. And if you see Mr Biscoe to be the pander of the lusts of the Defendant, give him not a farthing, but give the Defendant your verdict. But, on the contrary, if you shall be of the opinion that the Plaintiff was put off his guard, by pretended friendship, and that he has been robbed of his domestic comforts by the foulest conspiracy, I think no damages but Ten Thousand Pounds will satisfy the fair calls which Mr Biscoe makes on your honours and your consciences for justice.[3]

In the end, the jury decided that the truth was somewhere in the middle: the husband and the lover must share the blame. Their verdict was in favour of Joseph Biscoe, but he received only half of the £10,000 he had sought. Yet for Susanna, the price was much higher. Her decision to leave her daughter when she eloped from Shoreham meant that she could never again live with Mary, and the little girl was raised by her father. Joseph himself eventually had the union dissolved in 1795 and remarried four years later. Finally free to wed, Susanna and Gordon did so and remained together for the rest of Gordon's life. He predeceased Susanna in 1826, and she remained faithful to his memory until her death thirteen years later, never taking another husband.

---

3. Ibid., p.74.

The Prince of Scandal

In which Prinny romps his way to infamy...

> A more contemptible, cowardly, selfish, unfeeling dog does not exist ... There have been good and wise kings but not many of them ... and this I believe to be one of the worst.[1]

When Charles Greville, Clerk to the Privy Council, confided his scathing opinion of King George IV to his diary, he was echoing the opinion of much of the nation. Whether you know him as the Prince of Wales, the Prince Regent, Prinny or George IV, few monarchs have been more unapologetically scandalous than this one. His adventures could fill a whole volume,[2] but this is a whistle-stop tour of his most shocking greatest hits.

George was the eldest son of George III and Queen Charlotte, but despite his privileged birth, his childhood was anything but pampered. A strict educational regime and his father's refusal to let him follow his dreams of a military career fostered a sense of rebellion in the young royal that would govern his entire life. He loved excess, spending his father's money and partying in the limelight, and he revelled in the constant stream of adoring ladies that flocked in his wake.

When he was just a teen, George pursued Mary Hamilton, his sisters' governess, with a fervour that bordered on obsessive. Mary didn't want to know, but she had to put up with the prince's unwanted adoration, powerless to do anything but continually and politely – more politely

---

1. Baker, Kenneth (2005). 'George IV: A Sketch'. *History Today*. 55 (10): pp.30–36.
2. For the full story of this eyebrow-raising king, see my books, *Kings of Georgian Britain* and *The Wives of George IV: The Secret Bride & The Scorned Princess*, both published by Pen & Sword.

than he deserved – remind him that she simply wasn't interested. George wouldn't take no for an answer until, at the age of 17, he found a woman who was willing to indulge his spoiled, self-aggrandising whims.

She was Mary Robinson, a Bristolian actress who had already lived through enough drama to last a lifetime. When Mary's mother married her off in her teens, she lost a promising opportunity to train as an actress under the tutelage of David Garrick. Even worse, her deadbeat husband's debts landed them both in prison, but when Mary emerged, she headed straight to the stage and hit the big time. Mary made a name for herself that resulted in her winning top billing in a production of *A Winter's Tale*, which was being presented as a royal command performance. Sat beside his parents in the royal box, the Prince of Wales fell for Mary at first sight and swiftly offered her the position of mistress. She was five years his senior and well able to deal with stage door Johnnies, but he was a different sort of paramour altogether. The prince was rich, celebrated and dazzling, and he offered her the chance to escape her no-good husband once and for all – or so Mary hoped.

Mary and George began to exchange love notes, signing themselves as Perdita and Florizel respectively, the names of the lovers in *A Winter's Tale*. Mary was charmed by the prince, but she resisted his entreaties to disguise herself as a man and sneak into his home. Instead, she agreed to a stolen moonlit meeting chaperoned by Viscount Malden and the Duke of York, and it was at this meeting that the couple acknowledged their feelings for one another. When George repeated his offer of the position of official mistress and a payment of £20,000 to seal the deal, Mary took it. Wrongly believing George to be a man of his word, she accepted an IOU for the money. Unsurprisingly, the cash never materialised. Mary's decision to become the prince's mistress finished her marriage and career with a stroke, but it launched her into superstardom. Already a familiar figure in the press, Mary was about to go stratospheric.

There you shall see the famous Perdita of Drury-Lane, sitting at the play-house in the side box opposite the P— of W—. Look how wantonly she looks, thinking, Gracious Sir! Please to bestow one — upon a poor woman! Ho! Ho! Fine farce flow![3]

---

3. *Morning Post and Daily Advertiser.* 9 August 1780; issue 2431.

Mary's short time at the side of the Prince of Wales was spent in secluded midnight walks in the grounds at Kew, romping in the royal bedroom or carousing in the ballrooms of high society. They were celebrated and scandalous in equal measure, and her infamy reached such heights that the queen herself asked Mary to leave the theatre when the two women found themselves in the same audience.

Mary was the prince's first mistress, so perhaps we shouldn't be too hard on her for believing his breathless declarations of love. She and the rest of the world had yet to realise that the Prince of Wales loved only what he could not have. Once a woman swooned into his arms, she lost her lustre very quickly indeed, and so it proved for Mary Robinson. George didn't exactly dump her; he simply started to behave as though she didn't exist and went out on the town with other women, whilst Mary was left at home to count her rapidly disappearing money. Worse still, Mary's popularity as an actress evaporated along with her career when she gave up the stage to be a mistress, and now the press went for her with all guns blazing. Painted as a schemer who was hungry for money and had set out to ensnare the young prince, her life began to spiral.

Things came to a head a little more than a year after the affair began. With a note that said simply, 'we must meet no more,' the Prince of Wales moved on. Abandoned with neither her career nor her promised £20,000, Mary was adrift, left to pay for a lifestyle that she couldn't hope to afford. She turned to blackmail, telling the prince that she would publish his love letters unless she received her money. But she little expected that the king himself would get involved.

Horrified at the prospect of such an embarrassment, George III sent Colonel George Hotham to negotiate with Lord Malden, who was representing Mary. Malden explained that Mary needed at least £5,000 to satisfy her creditors, and Hotham agreed to pay the sum on behalf of the monarch, on the understanding that all the letters would be returned to him before the money changed hands. As an inducement, a further consideration of £500 a year for life would be paid to Mary Robinson.

Mary's reputation was gleefully destroyed by the press, though she would later enjoy considerable recognition as a poet in the difficult years that followed. She still had one last jab of the knife up her sleeve, and London thrilled to rumours that the prince's abilities as a lover lagged a long way behind his ability to spend money. He was impotent, they laughed, and that's all there was to it.

The Prince of Wales went through women at a rate of knots, but the only woman who he seems to have truly loved, and who loved him in return, was a twice-widowed Roman Catholic named Maria Fitzherbert. Once again, this was not a relationship that could have led to marriage, for the children of any monarch or heir who married a Catholic would be exempt from the line of succession. George was never one for rules, though.

When George met Maria at the opera, he was smitten, but the wealthy, respectable widow held her faith dear. She wasn't about to sacrifice her reputation for the whims of a prince whose love life was, by now, occupying multiple column inches. Just as he had done when chasing Mary Hamilton, George went into overdrive. He pursued Maria, snagging the seat next to her at events and social occasions, and turning up at her house to beat on the door if she dared to decline an invitation. Unlike Mary Hamilton, however, Maria Fitzherbert's resolve didn't strengthen. Instead, it began to weaken.

Things came to a head late one night when two representatives of the prince arrived at Maria's home and told her that George had attempted suicide and was unlikely to see the dawn. The prince's dying wish was to see Mrs Fitzherbert. Chaperoned by the dazzling Georgiana, Duchess of Devonshire, Maria agreed to visit the Prince of Wales on his deathbed, and the women set out into the night for Carlton House.

In the prince's opulent bedchamber, the heir to the throne was pale beneath his blankets. He was wrapped in bloodstained bandages and when he welcomed Maria and Georgiana, his voice was weak and faltering. It took him all his remaining strength to ask if Maria would accept a ring from him, as one final act of kindness to a dying man. Despite the duchess's reservations, Maria said yes and Georgiana reluctantly agreed to loan the couple a ring of her own.

No sooner did George slip the ring onto Maria's finger than he declared that a miracle had happened. His wounds were healed, and all because Mrs Fitzherbert had agreed to his proposal. Maria was horrified at his ruse and fled with Georgiana. After the two women had composed a sworn statement rejecting the very notion of a betrothal, Maria set off on an extended trip to Europe. She was determined never to see the Prince of Wales again.

George pursued Maria across the continent by proxy. Though George III refused permission for his debt-ridden son to travel, George sent letters, representatives and expensive gifts after Maria. She rather enjoyed the attention and, bit by bit, began to capitulate until she and the prince were exchanging adoring notes. Despite Maria's encouragement, she remained immovable on the matter of becoming a mistress. It wasn't her public image that bothered her as much as her faith. Maria's devout Catholic beliefs would simply not allow her to be anything but a wife, and she knew that marriage between the heir to the throne and a Roman Catholic commoner was an impossibility.

But the Prince of Wales didn't care for impossibilities. He gave Maria his word that he would marry her if she came home to England, and come home she did. The couple were wed in December 1785 in a secret ceremony that took place in Maria's Mayfair drawing room. The marriage was entirely without legal foundation, but it satisfied Maria's need to be married in the eyes of the Lord. From this point on, Maria became the unofficial queen of society at the side of her glamorous, celebrated husband. Though the king and queen were unsettled by scandalous rumours that the couple were more than lovers, they had to acknowledge that Maria Fitzherbert had been good for their eldest boy. The profligate, flighty prince seemed to settle down when he was with Mrs Fitzherbert, and his wild spending and even wilder living settled too.

The couple's undoing was money. George's debts hadn't gone away, and he needed a miracle to pay off his creditors. When he asked his friend, Charles James Fox, for help, Fox told him that there would be no payout from Parliament as long as rumours of an illegal marriage were doing the rounds. George was faced with a difficult decision; did he remain loyal to the woman who loved him and try to curb his spending, or did he renounce her in public, thus securing an end to his financial woes whilst breaking Maria's heart?

He chose the latter and authorised Fox to tell the House of Commons that there had been no marriage. Though Maria's name wasn't mentioned in the debate, when she heard what had happened, she was devastated. She was more devastated still when the Prince of Wales pocketed a fat payment from Parliament and headed off into the sunset to sow some more wild oats.

George and Maria were on and off for years, but she ultimately called a final halt to their tumultuous relationship many years later. By then the Prince of Wales had married and become estranged from his official and equally scandalous royal bride, and enjoyed a whole stack of lovers. His final misstep with Mrs Fitzherbert was placing her on a distant table at a society function 'according to her rank'. That was the last straw, and the couple was done for good. Yet decades later, when all was said and done, George was buried with Mrs Fitzherbert's miniature portrait around his neck and left everything he had to his secret wife. Maria never married again and remained loyal to the husband who had broken her heart to the end of her days.

But those sad events were still a long way off, and the Prince of Wales still had a lot of scandals to enjoy. Perhaps surprisingly, the biggest of them all came thanks to the one act that was supposed to make him respectable. Desperate for money, he capitulated to the king's demands that he should marry his cousin, Caroline of Brunswick.[4] The two were ill-matched from the off, and a drunken George wept through the ceremony before collapsing on the bedroom floor on his wedding night. Yet he must have woken up at some point because, nine months later, George and Caroline became parents to their only child, Princess Charlotte of Wales.

Hot on the heels of the birth came the separation of the Prince and Princess of Wales. Caroline of Brunswick moved into her own residence and began to entertain her estranged husband's political opponents. She revelled in the scandalous stories that were spread of her drunken parlour games and, before long, had bedded a few politicos just for good

---

4. I tell the whole sorry story in my book, *The Wives of George IV: The Secret Bride & The Scorned Princess*. (Pen and Sword, 2021)

measure. It's little wonder that George's fury at his perceived humiliation resulted in the supposedly secret Delicate Investigation of 1806, which aimed to establish whether a little boy that Caroline was raising was the illegitimate result of her adultery. Eventually, it was proven that he was actually a charity child whom the philanthropic princess had taken into her home.

The war of attrition between the prince and princess rumbled on for years, but when Caroline took off for Europe as her estranged husband settled into power as the Prince Regent, things reached a head. George became determined to prove a case of adultery against his wife and thus achieve his greatest ambition: divorce.

Caroline, meanwhile, was happily kicking up her heels in Italy with her chamberlain and lover, Bartolomeo Pergami. She had received news of her daughter Charlotte's pregnancy with delight and eagerly waited to be a grandmother. Instead, Charlotte died soon after she delivered a stillborn baby, and nobody thought to tell her mother. Caroline found out quite by accident when the prince's messenger passed close to her Italian residence and dropped the terrible bombshell.

It's hard to imagine how horrific it must have been for Caroline to receive the news of her daughter's death by accident, and she became determined to avenge herself on her hated husband. Her opportunity came with the death of King George III in January 1820. Now Caroline's spouse was king, and she was his queen. And she was going to milk it for all it was worth.

George greeted the return of his unwanted queen in 1820 with the biggest scandal the royal family had faced in years: the Pains and Penalties Bill. The bill placed the queen on trial for adultery in the House of Lords, and the stakes were high. If she was found guilty, she would be stripped of her titles, rank and privilege, and her marriage would be over. If she won the case, her husband's humiliation would be boundless.

The trial was the hottest talking point in London, and radicals flocked to rally round Caroline. She became a symbolic figurehead of the hatred the deprived population felt towards her spendthrift, hedonist husband. Henry Brougham was the queen's formidable representative for the defence, and he took the prince's case apart with all the skill of a surgeon wielding a scalpel. As the chamber of the House of Lords and newspaper headlines alike thrilled to witness statements that dissected Caroline's love life, Brougham knew that he had a trump card yet to play. Facing eyewitness claims of Caroline and Pergami's shared beds and baths, and even an incident in which she was caught in a carriage with her hand down the Italian's breeches, Brougham simply reiterated that she had been ill-used and humiliated by a loathsome husband. Could anyone really begrudge her some friendship and fun once freed from his shackles?

George won the case by a hair, but the impact on the country had been devastating. Fearing riot and revolution, the case did not proceed to the Commons and the king's last hope of securing a divorce passed.

The final act of this drama came at Westminster Abbey, where Caroline had been warned on no account to attend her husband's coronation. Instead, she turned up early, humiliated as door after door remained barred to her. Once the darling of the people, now she was an unwanted distraction from a much-needed national party. Caroline retreated to her home and almost immediately fell ill. Within weeks, she was dead.

Almost a decade later, George IV followed his wife to the grave, loathed to the last. The final word about the inconstant monarch must go to *The Times*, which savaged the dandy king.

There never was an individual less regretted by his fellow-creatures than this deceased king. What eye has wept for him? What heart has heaved one throb of unmercenary sorrow? ... If he ever had a friend — a devoted friend in any rank of life — we protest that the name of him or her never reached us.[5]

5. Morison, Stanley (1935). *The History of the Times: 'The Thunderer' in the Making, 1785–1841*. London: The Times, p.268.

The Fool of Fonthill

In which a gentleman finds himself ejected from society...

Mr Beckford of Fonthill is at Paris — but he was not concerned about the *Lady*.[1]

William Beckford was a one-off in an era that was full of them. Known as the *Fool of Fonthill*, he was shunned by high society for his behaviour, but revelled in the rewards that only being a millionaire could bring. He established one of the finest art collections in Europe, built a breathtaking tower that stands to this day, and was responsible for magnificent architecture and Gothic fiction alike, but his was a life filled with the sort of scandal that would do more than raise eyebrows even today.

The Beckford family made their money from slavery, amassing a vast fortune that made Beckford's father the richest man in England. He had twice served as Lord Mayor of London and his son enjoyed every manner of privilege, including music lessons from Mozart. Beckford senior died when William was just 10 years old, and the little boy inherited the family fortune and a valuable portfolio of land in England and Jamaica. Now the richest gentleman in London was nothing but a child.

As befitted a wealthy young gentleman set for a life of model respectability, in 1782, Beckford undertook his Grand Tour. The following year he made an excellent marriage to Lady Margaret Gordon, but his heart rested elsewhere. Beckford was soon embroiled in an affair with Louisa Pitt, the wife of his cousin, but that wasn't what made him

---

1. *The World*. 5 January 1789; issue 630.

notorious. That dubious honour was reserved for an episode that would explode into infamy.

Several years before his wedding, Beckford had met the 10-year-old William Courtenay, future 9th Earl of Devon. Courtenay was eight years Beckford's junior and the older man soon came to know him by the affectionate nickname Kitty. By 1784 their relationship had grown beyond friendship and when Beckford saw a gossipy letter written by Courtenay about Louisa Pitt, he was apoplectic. Joseph Farington witnessed the episode and wrote in his diary that Beckford 'went to [Courtenay's] room, and horsewhipped him, which created a noise, and the door being opened, Courtenay was discovered in his shirt, and Beckford in some posture or other – Strange story.'[2]

Courtenay's uncle – and Beckford's political enemy – Alexander Wedderburn, Lord Loughborough, lost no time in telling the press all about the episode. This was a time when sodomy was punishable by death, and Loughborough was perfectly happy to frame the bizarre quarrel in a manner that clearly hinted at a sexual tryst, without explicitly claiming that one taken place. It was enough to destroy Beckford's reputation, despite his efforts to weather the storm and rescue his nascent political career. King George III was so disgusted that he personally vetoed Beckford's chance of getting a peerage, but still Beckford wouldn't be cowed.

With Courtenay and Beckford's relationship splashed across the papers, one might have expected Beckford to go into hiding. He did no such thing. Instead, he and his wife, Margaret, initially continued to live in splendour at their Wiltshire seat of Fonthill Splendens. Only when things got too hot to handle did they take off for Europe, where they travelled with a magnificent entourage befitting a couple of such enormous wealth. Despite the scandal that had engulfed them, the Beckfords enjoyed a loving and devoted marriage that produced two children, but Beckford's interests lay elsewhere. During his wanderings, he authored *Vathek*, a fantasy story that took more than a suggestion of truth from his own life. In the book, Vathek builds a tower – just as

2. Bryson, Bill (2010). *At Home*. London: Transworld, p.219.

Beckford would later do – from which he can invade heaven itself. The caliph then attempts to sacrifice fifty local boys, but his attempts are thwarted and he is punished with an eternity in hell. For Beckford, it would become a blueprint.

When Margaret died in Switzerland as she delivered their second child, her widower was plunged into despair. The despondent Beckford returned to England and a secluded lifestyle at Fonthill, which he encircled with an enormous wall. What went on behind that fortress-like boundary had the gossips of England chattering like there was no tomorrow. They whispered excitedly of scandalous orgies, an all-male harem, and enough debauchery to make your eyes water. Behind the spiked walls, Beckford began to turn the fantasy of Vathek's life into reality, assembling a veritable harem of male servants to satisfy his every need.

Already shunned thanks to the Courtenay scandal, there was no going back now. Surrounded by his servants and an impressive library of pornography imported from the continent, Beckford pressed on with his collapsing fantasy. Not content with trying to conjure Vathek's sexual excesses into reality, he began construction on the perfect place in which to act them out: a magnificent Gothic cathedral named Fonthill Abbey. Overseen by architect James Wyatt, the project proved ruinously expensive and Beckford's fortune began to dwindle even as the abbey spire rose to 300 feet, towering ominously over the surrounding land. When Fonthill Abbey was officially unveiled in 1800, Emma Hamilton and Nelson were Beckford's guests of honour, but they were among a scant number of privileged attendees who were offered a glimpse behind the curtain into Vathek's world. Few people were afforded entry to the abbey's mysterious chambers and, for those on the outside, it became a symbol of sin, a temple of decadence where the most outrageous excesses were practised with abandon.

Yet behind those spiked walls, even debauchery began to lose its sparkle. The so-called harem was not made up of fictional beings whom Beckford could shape to his every whim, but of real people. That their company soon began to grow wearisome is evident by the nicknames that Beckford gave his companions as he whiled away the long and cold weeks of winter in his isolated hideaway.

'Nature and the human society round me are like the grave,' wrote the man who had once travelled Europe in such style that he was mistaken for a visiting emperor. 'There is pale Ambrose, infamous *Poupée*, horrid Ghoul, insipid Mme Bion, cadaverous Nicobuse, the portentous dwarf, frigid "Silence", and Salisbury Plain.'[3] Mourning his seclusion, Beckford speculated on the possibility of encouraging more young men to join him at Fonthill, before he became 'of so dark and extravagant a humour, so harsh and evil-tempered, that in tormenting everything which I see and which touches me I shall end up by tormenting myself to death. Countess Pox, more than half dead, fills me with disgust and pity.[4] But Beckford could never go back to the life he had known. His involvement with the young Courtenay and the rumoured escapades at Fonthill Abbey had ended his life as anything but an exile.

Beckford did occasionally venture out of his isolated sanctuary and visit London in a search for new lovers, but his lifestyle was unrecognisable from what it had once been. Eventually, the seclusion and expense of Fonthill Abbey began to weigh on its owner's spirits and finances. His fantasy life had proved to be just that, and the reality of the situation forced Beckford to sell not only the building, but also a large part of the extensive and priceless art collection that was housed there. The sale raised £300,000 and Beckford departed his grand folly for Bath, where he would soon conceive of yet another tower. This later structure still stands today, but Fonthill Abbey was not so lucky. The 300-foot-tall abbey tower collapsed in 1825, just three years after it was sold, and demolished the building with it. Miraculously, nobody was injured, but little remains of the folly of Fonthill today.

William Courtenay, the youth with whom Beckford had been so scandalously linked, fared little better. Unlike Beckford, who shut himself away behind spiked walls, Courtenay made no mystery of his sexual orientation. Though he was tireless in his philanthropic endeavours, his lifestyle was expensive, flamboyantly unapologetic and,

---

3. Alexander, Boyd (ed.) (1957). *Life at Fonthill, 1807–1822*. London: Rupert Hart-Davis Ltd, p.142.
4. Ibid., p.111.

for the time, shocking. When a warrant was issued for his arrest on charges of 'unnatural crimes', Courtenay left England. He travelled through America and France, and remained in exile for more than two decades. Kitty didn't even return when he became Earl of Devon, thanks to the efforts of a family historian who realised that the dormant title was legitimately Courtenay's.

Beckford died in Bath in 1844 at the age of 83, long considered a harmless eccentric as opposed to a real-world Vathek. Courtenay predeceased him by nearly a decade and died in his adopted home of Paris. The late Earl of Devon was mourned not only by his friends, but by the tenants who lived on his estates and loved their generous, eccentric benefactor to the end.

A Whisper of Scandal: Wellington's Wit

Henry Wellesley, 1st Baron Cowley, and brother to the Duke of Wellington, lost his wife Charlotte to Henry Paget, the married Earl of Uxbridge. When Paget served under Wellington at Waterloo, the Iron Duke commented wryly, 'Lord Uxbridge has the reputation of running away with everybody he can. I'll take good care he don't run away with me.'

Emma and the Heart of Oak

In which a hero loses his heart...

> The German State Painter, we are assured, is drawing Lady HAMILTON and Lord NELSON at *full length, together.* An Irish correspondent hopes the artist will have the delicacy enough to put Sir WILLIAM *between* them.[1]

There are some lovers who have become forever linked in the minds of the public. Antony and Cleopatra, Romeo and Juliet... and Lord Nelson and Lady Hamilton. As tragic historical romances go, it's one of the classics, and there's little surprise that it caused a sensation.

There were more than two players in the story of Nelson and Emma, besides the leading lights. Chief among the supporting cast was Sir William Hamilton, the British ambassador to the Kingdom of Naples and thirty-five years his wife's senior. Opposite him was Frances, Lady Nelson, the woman whom history would have us believe drove her husband into the arms of his adoring mistress. As far as stories go, it's as much soap opera as it is national news, and it's quintessentially Georgian.

Amy Lyon was born in 1765 in Cheshire. Her blacksmith father died soon after her birth, and Amy was raised by her mother and grandmother. By the time she was 12, young Amy was in London, and three years later she met Sir Henry Featherstonhaugh, a favourite of the Prince of Wales, and known to his friends as Harry. Amy became Harry's mistress, as well as hostess at his glittering and wild parties where she supposedly danced naked on the dinner table for the entertainment of her lover's

---

1. *Morning Post.* 15 September 1800; issue 9990.

friends. The life she lived was a world away from her destitute Cheshire childhood, yet though her surroundings were luxurious, Sir Harry was far from attentive. Once Amy's novelty had worn off, she found herself alone as her patron caroused with his wealthy pals. It was little wonder that she began to see more and more of Sir Charles Greville, a member of Harry's set whose quiet life left him plenty of free time to lavish on Amy. When she fell pregnant by Sir Harry in 1781, he threw her out. As soon as he did so, Sir Charles took her in as *his* mistress, on condition that her child, Emma Carew, be fostered out. Just 16 and already used and abandoned by a rich man, Amy complied.

Life with Greville was completely unlike the wild times that Amy had known at Uppark, Sir Harry's country estate. Hidden away in a small house near London, she acceded to Greville's request that she change her name to Mrs Emma Hart, which offered a façade of respectability. Emma even had her mother along to act as chaperone, ensuring that the arrangement stayed as respectable as it possibly could. Greville wouldn't let Emma meet his friends until she had improved her elocution and gained an education, and social visits were out of the question. It was a cloistered, stifling experience.

But Greville had reckoned without Emma's magnetic ways. When he agreed to let her sit for a portrait by his friend, George Romney, he inadvertently gave her just the break she needed. Romney was fascinated by the beautiful young woman and she became his muse, sitting for dozens of sketches and paintings that took society by storm. Emma was on the up.

Her patron, Sir Charles Greville, had never wanted a public affair and, as Emma's celebrity soared, he withdrew from her. Faced with a choice between marriage to a rich young lady or keeping Emma on as a mistress, he chose the former. As though she was a piece of property, Greville passed her onto his uncle, Sir William Hamilton, offering him a guarantee that he would take her back one day.

The recently widowed Hamilton regarded Emma as one more beautiful trinket to add to his collection and happily accepted her as his mistress. When Greville told Emma that she would be holidaying in Naples, she had no idea that it was a permanent arrangement. Instead,

Greville assured her that he would be away on business in Scotland and that she would enjoy a trip to Naples far more than tagging along with him. When Emma set off for the continent, she didn't even know that she had been passed on to another man. Her life offers an eye-opening glimpse into the realities of life for a woman of the era, shuffled from man to man without much of a say in her own fate.

When Emma arrived in Naples on her twenty-first birthday, she learned for the first time that she had been loaned out to Sir William Hamilton. Despite her misgivings, she was still convinced that she would be going home once Greville's Scottish business was concluded. Only after several months of asking when that would be did Emma realise that Greville had no intention of ever seeing her again. Emma was furious and became determined not to enjoy her life in Naples at all, but the social whirl and nightly parties, not to mention Sir William's gentlemanly attentions, soon changed her mind. Far from regarding her as a mistress of convenience, there simply to tend to his needs and play hostess at his parties, Sir William fell in love. He and Emma were married in London on 6 September 1791: the bride was 26 and the groom, 60.

In Naples, Emma was just as celebrated as she had been in London. She befriended royalty and became famed for her attitudes, *tableaux vivants*, in which the young woman would pose as sculptures or paintings. As she postured in diaphanous shawls and loose dresses, or sometimes nothing at all, Emma's guests would be charged with guessing who she was portraying, and her love of exotically draped gowns set off a trend right across Europe. Even scandalous rumours regarding the intimacy of her friendship with Queen Maria Caroline of Naples couldn't dent Emma's celebrity – it just made her more famous than ever. Life seemed to be close to perfect, but no matter how much Emma begged, there was one thing that Sir William would never do: he would not permit Emma's daughter to live with them, and she remained separated from her mother.

The first meeting between Lady Hamilton and Nelson came in 1793 when Nelson visited Naples to gather reinforcements for the Royal Navy's Mediterranean campaign. By this point, Nelson had been

married to Francis 'Fanny' Nisbet for several years, and few wives were as devoted as she.

Fanny was already a widow when she met Nelson in Nevis, the country of her birth. Nelson found the young widow enchanting company and married her in 1787. They made their home in Norfolk where Fanny cared for her ageing father-in-law as her husband forged his career at sea. Little did Fanny suspect that just as Nelson had sailed into Nevis and lost his heart to her, so too would he sail into Naples and fall for Emma Hamilton.

The first meeting between Emma and Nelson was not a case of love at first sight, but given what came later, it's easy to imagine that there must have been a mutual attraction. Five years passed before Nelson returned to Naples a hero, following his victory at the Battle of the Nile. Emma was still as fond of him as she had ever been, and when she learned that Nelson would stay with her and Sir William at the Palazzo Sessa, she was overjoyed.

Emma set about making herself indispensable to Britain's favourite hero, acting as his nurse, his secretary and his translator. Somewhere along the line, that arrangement became more intimate, and after Emma threw an extravagant party to honour Nelson's fortieth birthday, the couple became lovers. Sir William Hamilton knew precisely what was going on and, perhaps surprisingly, tolerated it without complaint. By the time Emma, Sir William and Nelson returned to England together in 1800, Emma was pregnant by her lover, who was ignorant of the child she already had. Nelson and the Hamiltons all took rooms at Nerot's Hotel, and when Fanny and her father-in-law arrived to welcome Nelson home, she was horrified to see that Emma was visibly with child. There was no question in her mind who the baby's father was.

With gossip linking the glamorous artist's muse to the Royal Navy's poster boy spreading like wildfire, it was only a matter of time before the affair became public knowledge. When it did, Fanny was devastated. Unlike Sir William, she wasn't willing to meekly step back for her rival, but nor was she the trendsetter and darling of the day: that role belonged to Lady Hamilton. Nelson made no secret of the fact that he preferred his mistress to his wife, and he began not only to neglect Fanny, but

to behave with cruel indifference towards her whenever he couldn't be with his beloved Emma. Still Fanny tried to win her husband back, culminating with a disastrous and ill-timed ultimatum that she delivered on the very day that he prepared to go back to sea.

Fanny told Nelson that he must choose once and for all: his mistress or his wife. In the last days of 1800, he told her, 'I love you sincerely but I cannot forget my obligations to Lady Hamilton, or speak of her otherwise than with affection and admiration.'[2] He had made his decision and sought a formal separation. Nelson would never reconcile with Fanny. As Fanny struggled to accept the end of her marriage, Nelson assured Emma that she was his wife, 'in my eyes and in the face of heaven'.

Horatia Nelson was born on 29 June 1801 and she was presented to the world as the orphaned goddaughter of Emma and Nelson. As the darling of the press and public, Emma courted adoration that the apparently dour and unemotional Fanny could not. Emma was a trendsetter whose every move was chronicled in acres of newsprint, and the public couldn't get enough of her. Nelson and Emma continually corresponded when he was at sea, and when he returned, he purchased Merton Place near Wimbledon, which Emma intended to convert into a shrine to her lover. Emma and William Hamilton moved into Merton Place with Nelson, where they lived in what some interpreted as an unapologetic ménage à trois, but which Sir William insisted was merely a happily platonic arrangement. Even this wasn't enough to turn public opinion against Emma, who had one last wish: to be reunited with the little girl she had been forced to give up. When she finally confessed the existence of Emma Carew to Nelson, he showed sensitivity and understanding. He agreed to support her financially and invited the young lady to join them at Merton Place for a holiday. For the first time, one of Emma's lovers had accepted her eldest child. Emma Hamilton seemed to have it all at last.

Everything changed with the death of Sir William in 1803. No longer cushioned by the dubious respectability afforded by her husband's

2. Jeaffreson, John Cordy (1888). *Lady Hamilton and Lord Nelson, Vol. II*. London: Hurst and Blackett, Limited, p.214.

presence at Merton Place, Emma moved into a nearby house. She hoped to preserve the façade of platonic friendship, even though she was pregnant again. Nelson left to face Napoleon just a month after the death of Sir William, and Emma awaited his return in an agony of loneliness. The couple's second child died within weeks of her birth, plunging Emma into despair that she tried to numb with alcohol and the thrill of the gaming tables. By now a wealthy widow, she received and rejected plenty of proposals, waiting for the return of Nelson instead. When it came, their reunion was brief, but the couple took the opportunity to undergo a quasi-marriage service, exchanging rings and promises of a shared future. After that, Nelson was off again, into the smoke and chaos of the Battle of Trafalgar.

Nelson was killed in action on 21 October 1805. Among his last words were a plea to Captain Hardy to 'take care of my dear Lady Hamilton', a request that was echoed in his will. His death plunged the nation into mourning, and none mourned more than Lady Emma Hamilton. She languished in bed in a deep depression, but there were more shocks to come. Nelson's will left almost everything to his brother, William, whilst Emma was to receive £2,000, Merton Place, and an annuity of £500. Despite having left a request that the government take care of Emma, as well as expressing a desire that she be invited to sing at his funeral, Nelson's last wishes were ignored. Though Emma had been generous to a fault with her lover's family, they did not return the favour, and William refused to pay her the £500 a year she was due.

Emma tried to keep up her lavish lifestyle, but it was soon impossible. Deep in debt, the only solution was to sell Merton Place. Emma resisted the sale with every fibre of her being and tried in vain to delay it by selling off her treasured mementoes of Nelson instead. Yet with every new report of her continued decline, public opinion turned against her a little more. The last vestiges of sympathy ran out when intimate letters between Emma and Nelson were published in 1814, and the blame fell on Emma.

Desperate to escape her creditors in England, Emma and Horatia fled for France in 1814, taking their last £50 with them. Yet even now,

Emma kept up the sham of a wealthy lifestyle, continuing to spend and live the high life as her debts became ever more extreme.

Once again Emma attempted to stave off her depression with alcohol and laudanum, but her dwindling funds forced her to take humble rooms on the Rue Française in Calais. She died there in 1815, aged 49. Fanny, meanwhile, remained faithful to Nelson until her death in 1831. To the end, she alone was recognised as Nelson's only widow.

Mr Long-Pole's Wicked Ways

In which an heiress makes a fatal decision…

> A spendthrift, a profligate, and gambler in his youth, [William Wellesley-Pole] became a debauchee in his manhood, and achieved the prime disgrace of being the second person whom the Courts of Chancery deprived of paternal rights, by withdrawing out of his care his children, whose early tastes and whose morals he wickedly endeavoured to corrupt, from a malicious desire to add to the agonies of their desolate and broken-hearted mother. Redeemed by no single fortune — adorned by no single grace — his life has gone out, even without a flicker of repentance.[1]

Catherine Tylney-Long was a woman who had it all. As the eldest surviving child of Sir James Tylney-Long, 7th Baronet, it was she who inherited his vast estates and immense wealth. Boasting a fortune of £300,000 (more than £25 million at the time of writing), an eye-watering property portfolio and estates that brought in £40,000 every year (£4 million today), she was the richest commoner in all of England. Known as the Wiltshire Heiress, Miss Tylney-Long was an eligible young lady indeed. When she took the air in Hyde Park, Lady Harriet Leveson-Gower thought 'it was droll to see Miss Long's admirers riding about her carriage as the guards do about the king's.'[2]

Thanks in no small part to her immense wealth, Catherine was one of society's most celebrated figures, but her popularity was also a testament

---

1. *Morning Chronicle.* 4 July 1857; issue 28247.
2. Leveson-Gower, F. (ed.) (1894). *Letters of Harriet Countess Granville, Vol I.* London: Longmans, Green, and Co, p.1.

to her unspoiled and likeable manner. Despite her great fortune and privilege, she was refreshingly down to earth, and the media and public loved her. In a world where newspapers, coffeehouse gossips and caricaturists shone a gleeful spotlight on the slightest failing in any public figure – especially the rich – the Wiltshire Heiress was content to simply be herself. Witty, unpretentious and good company, it should come as no surprise that Catherine had no shortage of admirers. Among them was William, Duke of Clarence, who would one day reign as King William IV. Though he was twenty-four years Catherine's senior, he fruitlessly hoped to woo her and prop up his dwindling coffers with her wealth. Yet as Lady Leveson-Gower knew, the Duke of Clarence was merely one in a legion of would-be suitors, all of whom had failed to catch the lady's eye. 'I left Miss,' says Lady LG, 'Refusing to the right and left.'[3] But she wouldn't refuse forever.

When Catherine rejected the Duke of Clarence's proposal, society was aghast. Her family encouraged her to accept, but she wouldn't budge. Catherine had her own ideas when it came to love, and when she set eyes on the handsome, dashing William Wellesley-Pole, she fell head over heels for one of the most desirable men in London. Elegant, fashionable and absurdly well connected, this 23-year-old gadabout dandy was the man of the moment. Though Wellesley-Pole was far from rich, his family tree more than made up for that. He was the nephew of the future Duke of Wellington, and son of the 3rd Earl of Mornington, from whom he would eventually inherit the title. On top of that, as a leading member of Beau Brummell's influential circle, he knew how to work his charms to devastating advantage.

Catherine and William met at a London gathering shortly after he had returned from a military and diplomatic tour across the continent. She was dazzled by his urbane and accomplished manner, and he sealed the deal by performing an impressive equestrian display at her coming-of-age fete. The most wealthy commoner in England was besotted with the swaggering gentleman of fashion. Surrounded as she was by men bowing and scraping in a bid to win her favour, the exciting, ever-so-

3. Ibid., p.5.

slightly forbidden charms of William Wellesley-Pole were exactly what Catherine was looking for.

For all that he was fashionable, William's reputation was anything but peerless. He was a rake and, with his empty purse doing nothing to curtail his rip-roaring ways, exactly the kind of fortune-seeker that Catherine's friends and family feared. William had a list of rumoured lovers as long as that of Catherine's would-be suitors, but he was fiercely jealous of anyone who sought to supplant him in her affections. William believed that he alone should be allowed to squire the heiress in the waltz, so when Lord Kilworth, later 3rd Earl Mount Cashell, danced a little too close, William challenged him to a duel. Though the matter was settled amicably and without bloodshed, it did little to impress his sceptical critics. Not only was Wellesley-Pole a fortune-hunter, they murmured, but he was a fortune-hunter with a reckless disregard for safety and an arrogant love of his own notoriety.

For a short time after the duel, Catherine's affections for her suitor cooled, but when Clarence came calling again, William swung into action. He won back Catherine's affections during a series of secret, unchaperoned and heated meetings that were a world away from the duke's stuffy, proper approaches. William finally sealed his claim to Catherine's heart when he chased away a stalker who had been harassing her for months, a feat that nobody else had been able to achieve. If that wasn't dashing enough, when Wellington's son – William's nephew – was taken ill at Broadstairs, William made a dramatic horseback dash to bring a doctor to the ailing child's bedside. Thanks to his quick thinking and tireless heroism, the little boy's life was saved. Tales of William's escapades gripped society and when he made his proposal to Catherine, she was quick to accept.

Marrying the richest commoner in England was no small matter, and Catherine's family insisted that a prenuptial agreement be drawn up that protected at least some of her assets. This was a considerable achievement in an age when a wife's entire assets became the property of her husband at marriage. The prenup gave Catherine sole control over approximately 50 per cent of her estates, and William direct control over the remaining 50 for his lifetime only, meaning he could sell nothing.

Catherine was also entitled to sole enjoyment of a generous yearly stipend of more than £10,000, though in reality, William helped himself to it instead. In keeping with the laws of the day, William had legal rights over the income and rents his wife's assets generated, and that amounted to a fortune. But she trusted him and he knew it.

With the papers signed, the glittering wedding ceremony took place at St James's in Piccadilly on 14 March 1812. Perhaps it was an omen that William had forgotten to purchase a ring, and a jeweller had to be whisked along to the church to save the day.

Once the couple were married, William changed his name to the eye-watering William Pole-Tylney-Long-Wellesley. Armed with his new moniker, he launched a political career, then, once Catherine was pregnant with the couple's first child, William got busy spending. The Pole-Tylney-Long-Wellesleys completely refurbished their grand residence at Wanstead House, where the Prince Regent was a regular visitor, but even as the public lapped up tales of their extravagant ways, things began to sour. There were rumours of infidelity on William's part, and Catherine realised too late that she had made the worst decision of her life.

In 1818, William gave up his safe parliamentary seat for St Ives to fight a seat in Wiltshire. Opposed by a local candidate who decried him as a man who was trying to buy his way to power, William had to spend an absolute fortune to secure the victory. With his parties, his spending and his unbridled love of the finer things in life, even the wealth he had acquired from his marriage was proving woefully inadequate to cover his outgoings, and he took drastic action. William began to borrow money and even mortgaged his portion of the marital estates, but still he couldn't hope to balance the books. In 1820 he resigned his parliamentary seat and, faced with a stint in a debtor's prison, he gathered up his wife and three children and fled for Paris. The family returned two years later when William's father was able to secure him a position as Gentleman Usher and Daily Waiter to George IV, an office that carried with it the sweetener of immunity from arrest for debt. Despite this, William's creditors continued to hound him and the Pole-Tylney-Long-Wellesleys were soon on the run in Europe again.

Let us stop for a moment to consider this dramatic and almost unbelievable fall from grace. That William was able to spend so much money in less than ten years is mind-blowing. It is a testament to the sheer selfishness of the man, whilst the way the laws of marriage disenfranchised women meant that Catherine had no mechanism to protect herself and the wealth she had brought into the relationship. One can scarcely imagine Catherine's despair when, in 1822, the contents of her beloved home at Wanstead were auctioned off. 25,000 copies of the sale catalogue were snapped up, and thousands of people visited to pick over the items on offer, but the £41,000 raised barely scratched the surface of William's debts. Protected from arrest he might be, but that didn't stop his creditors from hounding him for their money and he fled for the continent once more, leaving his father to untangle the mess. Even Wanstead wasn't safe. It was sold off and eventually demolished in 1825, erasing the once-magnificent home where Catherine had hoped to raise her own family in the same happy surroundings that she had known.

What might be even more surprising than William's far from heroic ability to spend money was the fact that, when the family arrived in Italy, Catherine was still loyal to her husband. She was happy in her new surroundings, no longer facing the shame of William's endless stream of creditors and still very much in love. When Catherine's mother died whilst the family was in Europe, she declared that William had been her rock. Of course, this being William, that loyalty wasn't reciprocated.

Among the Pole-Tylney-Long-Wellesleys' social circle in Naples were Helena Bligh and her husband Thomas, an officer of the Coldstream Guards. The couple were staying in Italy for the sake of Bligh's health and were dazzled by their famous friends. When William and Helena began an affair, Catherine finally found that she could no longer make excuses for her husband's appalling behaviour. The lovers made no secret of their liaisons and took *night excursions* together, supposedly to see the sights. In reality, they were merely excuses to be alone. There are probably few couples who can claim to have had sex on the slopes of Mount Vesuvius, but William boasted to his friends that he and Helena had done just that. Little wonder that he earned the mocking nickname, Mr Long-Pole.

When Thomas Bligh learned of his wife's behaviour, he threw her out. Unthinkably, William moved her into the home he shared with Catherine, and, at last, the wronged woman could stand it no more. She used the excuse of a trip to Florence to ask Helena to make alternative arrangements, but the affair continued. It was this that broke Catherine's already wounded heart. She begged William's parents to intervene, promising that she would finance Helena for life if she would only end her connection with William, but William was not to be dissuaded. He told Catherine that Helena was mad and, without his support, would kill herself. Needless to say, this was just another lie. What William wanted, he had to have.

Catherine fled for England, leaving William and Mrs Bligh to live it up in Paris. Confronted by the harsh realities of her sham marriage, Catherine warned her husband that if he dared come to England in the hope of winning her back, she would do all she could to obtain a divorce. Yet William was not about to be deterred and threatened to seize the couple's children, whom he would effectively hold to ransom to ensure that Catherine continued to bankroll him. Catherine's prenup gave her complete control over spending money of £11,000 per year, but William had always forced her to share that allowance with him. Now they were apart, she took back control of her personal allowance and refused to fund her husband's gallivanting in Paris. To add insult to injury, William had infected Catherine with a venereal disease. It was the final indignity.

When William invaded the London house where Catherine was staying and attempted to abduct their children, Catherine hid herself away in Richmond with her sisters. Desperate for a divorce and terrified of what he might do, she filed a bill that would make her youngsters wards of Chancery, thus protecting them from their father should any harm befall her. Comforted by the knowledge that her children were safe, in the autumn of 1825, the heiress who had once had the world at her feet fell dangerously ill. She died on 12 September at the age of just 35, a shadow of the happy, carefree young lady she had once been. Yet even after her death, Catherine knew no peace. The press launched into long soliloquies reflecting on her fate, whispering darkly that it should

be a warning to all wealthy women to take care, lest the same unhappy ending befall them too.

Following Catherine's death, William petitioned the Court of Chancery for custody of his children – and lost. Though he was not the first father to be denied his paternal rights in Chancery, he was the first to be denied custody of his children on the grounds that he was morally unfit. Instead, they were taken into the care of the Duke of Wellington. This was a blow to William not because of any feelings of paternal love, but because his greed was boundless. After Catherine's death, her money passed to her eldest son, and William hoped to seize both the child and the cash for himself. He was in the press again when Captain Bligh sued him for criminal conversation and won a settlement of £6,000. William, it seemed, simply couldn't stay out of the headlines.

Only in the years after he became a widower did William taste some of the bitter medicine which he had long deserved. Loathed and vilified for his behaviour, upon the death of George IV he was finally committed to the Fleet Prison after an attempt to abduct his daughter. Even his marriage to the former Mrs Bligh ended in scandal when he cheated on her with a maid. Needless to say, when the couple separated after reaching a financial arrangement, Helena saw none of the money that had been promised. Through all of this, William continued his political career and even managed to entice his middle child, James, to join him in a life of vice and dissipation. It was a small victory against Catherine's memory.

The profligate, shamed master of Wanstead House succeeded as Earl of Mornington in 1845, but the title bought precious few riches. Eventually, he was reduced to living on a meagre pension provided by his cousin, the 2nd Duke of Wellington, but it was a long way from the opulence he had once enjoyed. William died in his sorry lodgings in 1857. Few mourned his passing.

The Trials of Lady Caroline

In which a woman battles her demons in the glare of the spotlight...

Oh sweetest devel tis now my turn to write to you that you should burn.

> I'm mad
> that's bad
> I'm sad
> That's bad
> I'm mad
> That's mad.[1]

Few Regency names are as synonymous with scandal as that of Lady Caroline Lamb, who wrote the above lines at the tender age of 11. The woman who famously described Lord Byron as 'mad, bad and dangerous to know' has been painted as history's most extreme ex-girlfriend, and a person defined by the man she loved. Yet is that really how Lady Caroline Lamb deserves to be remembered?

Caroline Ponsonby[2] was born on 13 November 1785, the only daughter of Frederick Ponsonby, 3rd Earl of Bessborough, and Henrietta Spencer, sister of the celebrated Georgiana, Duchess of Devonshire. Her childhood was marred by her parents' unhappy and abusive marriage, and she was raised in a whirl of confusion, caught on the one hand between the misery unfolding at home and on the other by the glittering prizes of the Devonshire House set. It was little wonder that she was an

---

1. Douglass, Paul (2006). *The Whole Disgraceful Truth*. London: Palgrave Macmillan, p.7.
2. Lady Caroline was distantly related to Sarah Ponsonby, one half of the celebrated ladies of Llangollen.

unconventional girl, dressing in breeches and galloping from one mood to the next, caught in a world of daydreams. She was often left in the care of her grandmother, Lady Spencer, a bastion of the establishment who unsurprisingly found the little girl difficult to manage. They could not have been more different.

By the time Caroline made her society debut, she was ready to shine. Intelligent, witty and with the sort of gamine looks that earned her the nickname the Sprite, she was one of the most sought-after personalities in the ton. She was also temperamental and given to sudden rages, but for some people that just made her all the more captivating. Men were besotted by the mercurial young lady, and none more so than William Lamb, second son of Lord Melbourne. The attraction was mutual, but the lovers were star-crossed. Since William was only a younger brother, the strict social rules of the upper classes dictated that he couldn't propose to Caroline, whose standing was higher than his. A family tragedy in 1805 changed all that when William's elder brother – also the heir to the dukedom – died of tuberculosis. With William elevated to the position of heir apparent, he could finally propose to the dazzling Lady Caroline. The dazzling Lady Caroline was delighted to accept.

The first signs of trouble came when the marriage was barely minutes old. Caroline had been sick with excitement and agitated all day, but she became hysterical at the close of the wedding ceremony. Though she had to be carried from the room, her outburst only made her groom love her more. He was her fiercest protector, but even the most dedicated husband couldn't shield such a sensitive young woman from the world, and nor would Caroline have wished him to. She thrived on excitement, even as it wrung her out and left her reeling.

At first, the couple were happy, but their idyll couldn't last. The Lambs' first child, George, was born with severe learning disabilities and the decision to care for him at home placed a considerable strain on the couple. Understandably, the death of their second child, a daughter who lived less than 24 hours, further exacerbated the unhappy situation. On top of that, the Lambs couldn't have been more different to one another when it came to their temperaments. Caroline was fiery and dramatic and ready to fight any battle, but William longed for a quiet life that would give him the foundations he needed in order to focus on his political career. As their arguments grew more intense, their seemingly idyllic love fell apart.

William devoted himself in equal part to his love of flagellation and his political ambitions. He indulged in consensual spanking sessions with mistresses and took disturbing delight in birching the young women who worked in his household, yet it was his wife whose behaviour dominated the chattering drawing rooms of the ton. Politics and spanking left little time for Caroline, and she found herself in search of entertainment elsewhere. Where better to find adventure than in the person of the infamous Lord Byron?

Caroline became obsessed with Byron, at the time the most famous and feted man in the land, and she positively melted when he awarded her the affectionate diminutive of *Caro*. They began a passionate, violent affair, and made no effort to conceal it. William, placid as ever, was willing to let his wife indulge her fancies until she tired of them, but it was Byron whose passion blew out first. He turned away from the obsessive neediness of his Caro in favour of her friend, Lady Oxford, and the double betrayal shattered her. She burned Byron's gifts on a bonfire as children chanted a poem she had written to denounce her lover. When that didn't satisfy her, Caroline dressed her manservants in a livery that included buttons engraved with the warning, 'Ne crede Byron' – 'do not believe Byron'.

Resorting to ever more disturbing efforts to capture his attention, Caroline even sent Byron a clipping of her pubic hair. It was still wet with her blood. 'I cut the hair too close and bled more than you need,' she told him. Unsurprisingly, this didn't bring Byron running back to her arms. Even Caroline's mother took the poet's side wholeheartedly, leaving her feeling more alone than ever.

In an effort to help his wife forget her broken heart, William took Caroline to Ireland to convalesce, but she and Byron continued to correspond during the trip. Restless and disturbed, Caroline was utterly infatuated with her former lover, but he showed her no kindness. When she saw him dance with another woman at a ball, Caroline shattered the glass she was holding and sliced at her arms with the shards. Lady

Melbourne, Caroline's mother-in-law, had initially adored her husband's wife, but now her affection had turned to revulsion. Perhaps, she suggested, Lady Caroline Lamb should be locked away. Her husband wouldn't hear of it.

It was when Caroline was at her most desperate that the ton turned its back on her. No matter how cruelly entertaining they found her despair, such publicly outrageous behaviour was more than they were willing to sanction. Byron, who revelled in the attention and Caroline's helpless adoration, coldly dismissed her self-inflicted injuries as theatre. 'Lady Caroline performed the dagger scene [from Macbeth],' he sniffingly commented when she cut herself. Yet even when publicly faced with his derision, Caro continued to try and win Byron back. She visited the poet's home in disguise as a page and scribbled 'Remember Me!' in the flyleaf of one of his books. His response has become infamous:

> Remember thee! Remember thee!;
> Till Lethe quench life's burning stream,
> Remorse and shame shall cling to thee,
> And haunt thee like a feverish dream!
>
> Remember thee! Ay, doubt it not.
> Thy husband too shall think of thee:
> By neither shalt thou be forgot,
> Thou false to him, thou fiend to me!

Caroline's fixation with Byron came to define her and to dominate her every conscious moment. By the time Byron left England in 1816, the scandal around the affair had died down, but Caro still couldn't forget him, nor forgive the circle that had rejected her. She poured her energies into a novel and *Glenarvon* brought her blazing back into the spotlight. If nothing else, history should remember Caroline Lamb as a serious literary talent. Her single-minded pursuit of Lord Byron merely served to derail a career that might have shone.

Glenarvon was a novel set in high society that featured a thinly-veiled Byron and Lady Caroline as the lead characters. Around them was a cast of supporting players who were clearly and unashamedly based on real people, all of whom had no difficulty in recognising themselves. They also knew exactly who the supposedly anonymous author was.

The fallout was tremendous. Lady Jersey rescinded Caroline's highly prized Almack's voucher, and even the long-suffering William seemed to have reached the point of no return. He initially intended to separate from his wife for good, but when he realised how isolated she was becoming, he relented. Over the years that followed, both Caroline and William took many lovers, and they briefly separated in 1825, but they always reunited eventually. To the end of her life, William was his wife's protector. 'We will stand or fall together,' he promised.

Assailed by drama after drama, some of her own making, it was Byron's death that hit Caroline hardest of all, but eventually freed her too. She fell into a complete mental collapse and was threatened with a straitjacket on more than one occasion. Growing ever more reclusive, Caroline lost herself in booze and laudanum, and her rages and hysterical fits became daily occurrences. She hit rock bottom and it was there, as she came to terms with Byron's death, that she gradually began to turn the corner. In his memoirs, Byron had rejected Caroline as just another nobody who was desperate to touch his flame, but now he was no longer in the world, no longer living his life without her, Caroline could finally move on from her obsession. Her nerves recovered, her rages grew less frequent and she was content at last in the company of her husband. When Caroline fell sick with what would be a fatal illness, her only instruction was telling. 'Send for William,' she begged. 'He is the only person who has never failed me.'

Lady Caroline Lamb died on 26 January 1828. Her husband, the future prime minister of the United Kingdom and trusted mentor to the young Queen Victoria, was by her side. A decade later, he too was embroiled in a very public scandal, when he was sued for criminal conversation by George Chapple Norton over allegations that Norton's wife, Caroline, had been sleeping with the then prime minister. After little more than a week, the case was thrown out and Melbourne's career was saved. His fame has endured as a statesman, whilst his wife is remembered as Byron's obsessive, troubled lover. Yet in her writing, we see the true

Lady Caroline Lamb – arch, witty and more than able to skewer those who judged her so harshly.

A Whisper of Scandal: Mr Wesley's Morals

Known to some as the English Mozart, Samuel Wesley initially refused to marry the woman he loved because he believed that by having sex, they had sealed their commitment for good. A few years after he finally dragged himself to the altar, the middle-aged composer abandoned his wife for a teenage servant. Luckily for him, his Freemason interests ensured that he was never without work or influential friends, regardless of his antics.

The Million Pound Scandal

In which a gentleman and his sister-in-law raise eyebrows...

Sir H[enry], who seemed unwilling to depart, at length threw himself upon his knees before Lady R[osebery], and embracing her knees, exclaimed, 'Will you forgive me?' ... He then asked for his pistols, saying he might meet with strange people ... ran to the window and jumped out.[1]

In 1814 the drawing rooms of high society were alive with a particularly red-hot topic of conversation: the criminal conversation trial brought by the Earl of Rosebery against Sir Henry Mildmay. From guns to daring escapes and plenty of sex, it had everything the gossips relished. And most scandalous of all, the lovers were in-laws.

Sir Henry St John-Mildmay, 4th Baronet, was a dandy and a politician. One of the most fashionable men in London, he was noted for his exquisite taste, his wealth and his love of ostentatiously displaying both. A friend of Beau Brummell and the Prince Regent alike – until Prinny famously cut him – where Mildmay and his set went, everyone wanted to follow.

In 1809 Sir Henry married Charlotte Bouverie and, within the first year of their marriage, she fell pregnant. Charlotte died delivering a healthy baby boy mere days before the couple's first wedding anniversary, leaving Mildmay and her sister, Harriet, bereft. Harriet was comforted in her grief by her husband, Archibald Primrose, 4th Earl of Rosebery, but little could he guess where the loss of his sister-in-law would eventually lead.

1. Anonymous (1814). *The Scots Magazine, and Edinburgh Literary Miscellany, Vol. LXXVI*. Edinburgh: Archibald Constable and Company, p.927.

As the widower and the grieving sister, herself the mother of four children, sought solace together, their mutual misery gradually turned into something rather more passionate. Sir Henry and Lady Harriet began an affair that wasn't just scandalous but skirted with illegality too. Under British law, no man could marry the sister of his late wife, just as no woman could marry the brother of her late husband. Sex, of course, didn't concern itself with such trivialities.

When Lord Rosebery learned about the affair, he promptly sued Sir Henry for criminal conversation and 'alienating his wife's affections'. The torrid details were splashed all over the press and readers lapped it up. Given Sir Henry's wealth, Lord Rosebery inevitably demanded proper reparations, and a jury was convened to hear the charges and decide on an appropriate penalty.

At the trial Lady Harriet was presented as an unworldly innocent, married at 18 to a man who worshipped her. She was noted for her generosity and philanthropy, stated the Attorney General, Sir William Garrow, and she would never have swerved from the path of good had she not been seduced into vice by the manipulative Mildmay. To further compound matters, explained Garrow, Sir Henry and Lord Rosebery were good friends before the affair, and the latter had been a rock for the former on the death of his wife. It appeared that Sir Henry had exploited that close friendship to carry out his seduction, as he had been privy to the information that Lady Harriet would be alone whilst her husband visited his dangerously ill father in Scotland. It was then, claimed Garrow, that Sir Henry made his move.

Once Lord Rosebery returned home from Scotland, he found the previously serene Lady Harriet distracted and distant. Upon learning that Sir Henry had been a regular caller in his absence, Lord Rosebery concluded that his unwanted attentions must have unsettled Harriet and told Sir Henry that he was no longer welcome in the Rosebery home. He little suspected that things had already progressed far beyond friendly visits.

When the Primroses departed for a summer holiday in Edinburgh, Sir Henry gave chase in the guise of a sailor, and Lady Harriet hastened to his bed. It was here that they were discovered, and a search of their rooms turned up a cache of impassioned love letters that proved the affair was no flash in the pan.

Lord Rosebery was devastated by the double betrayal, and it was this devastation that was presented to the jury as the primary reason for awarding substantial damages. He was entirely innocent, they were told: a loving husband and father to four children who had been humiliated by the seduced Lady Harriet and his traitorous friend, time and again. Lady Harriet was debauched by Henry Mildmay, argued Garrow, and there was nothing that could be done about it: she was past saving. Indeed, Mildmay's letters to Harriet alluded to her coolness towards her husband and children, and were sympathetic towards the family even as he played his part in destroying it. Sir Henry even hoped to provoke a duel, in which he would not harm Lord Rosebery but merely best him. Then he would offer a solution – Lady Harriet could stay with her husband for the sake of appearances, but Sir Henry would enjoy unrestricted access to her. It was mindboggling stuff.

A procession of witnesses came forward to tell of stolen trysts and secret liaisons, and even of an armed Sir Henry stealing in and out of the house via a window like a romantic hero. The jury heard all about Lady Harriet's hysterics on her lover's departure, as well as her husband's hopeless efforts to win back her affection. It was a tale of co-dependency as much as love, with Lady Harriet and Sir Henry as needy and out of control as teenagers, and Henry Brougham's vigorous cross-questioning for the defence did little to dilute the impact the witness testimonies were having on the jury. Yet he did his best, arguing that Lord Rosebery would have preferred to keep his wife and avoid scandal, but it was she and her lover who continually poked the hornet's nest, as it were. Sir Henry was a lost soul, said Brougham, whose grief at the loss of his wife had caused him to act out of character and fall for Harriet, who was also out of her mind with sorrow. Nobody in this case sought to hurt anyone, Brougham assured the jury, and Sir Henry felt nothing but compassion for the man he had betrayed. It was merely an unfortunate affair of the heart.

The jury was not swayed. They awarded Lord Rosebery a record-breaking £15,000, approximately £1 million at the time of writing. Lord

Rosebery promptly divorced his wife and she and Sir Henry eloped to Württemberg, where they were married. Harriet and Henry had three children before her death in 1834. Sir Henry lived on for a further fourteen years until, plagued by financial worries, he took his own life.

A Whisper of Scandal: The Adventures of Lady Jane Digby

Lady Jane Digby was a sexual adventuress. After marrying the future Earl of Ellenborough, she embarked on a series of scandalous affairs that led to a widely publicised divorce. Her adventures took her through four marriages, intrigues with royalty, and across the continent to Greece, where she joined the War of Independence in support of her latest lover. Lady Jane eventually settled in Syria as the wife of Sheik Medjuel el Mezrab. There she divided her time between a nomadic desert tent and an opulent palace, as well as adding Arabic to the eight languages that she already spoke fluently. It was a life very well lived indeed.

Lady Blessington's Boys

In which a lady flees England to kick up her continental heels…

> All subjects are good in their way, provided they are sufficiently diversified; but scandal has something so piquant, — it is sort of cayenne to the mind, — that I confess I like it, particularly if the objects are one's particular friends.[1]

Margaret Power was born in 1789 at Knockbrit, County Tipperary, and she had to grow up fast. She was raised by a drunken father whose only priority when it came to his daughter was to get her married off and out of his hair. He achieved his aim when Margaret was just 15, hitching his distraught daughter to Captain Maurice St Leger Farmer. It proved to be a terrifying and miserable period in the girl's life as she found her new husband was subject to bouts of mental illness and violence, during which he would beat her black and blue or starve her until she could barely lift her head. Yet even as Margaret's body suffered, her spirit and will were as strong as her determination to escape. When Farmer was posted abroad, Margaret refused to go with him, no matter how hard he beat her. Instead, she took refuge with her family, where she endured a cold welcome. Even that was better than life with Farmer.

Margaret stayed under her parents' roof for several years, until she heard that her husband was due back in England. Fearing for her future and sure that she would be forced to return to him, Margaret accepted the overtures of sea captain Thomas Jenkins, who offered her sanctuary in the Dublin home he shared with his mother and siblings.

---

1. Blessington, Marguerite, Countess of (1836). *Conversations of Lord Byron with the Countess of Blessington*. Philadelphia: E.L. Carey & A. Hart, p.56.

Margaret stayed with Jenkins for five years and the couple travelled together, making no secret of their attachment to one another. Yet, as much as Margaret was affectionate towards Jenkins and valued his companionship, she never truly loved him. This was no grand passion, but an arrangement that suited both.

Jenkins introduced Margaret to Charles Gardiner, 1st Earl of Blessington, who was soon enchanted by her. Blessington was a widower with four children, and he was determined to marry Margaret as soon as she could get a divorce. Margaret was keen to accept and, once Lord Blessington had paid Captain Jenkins £10,000 for the dresses and other items she would bring with her, as well as for the care he had provided for the past five years, the deal was done. Margaret left Jenkins on good terms and moved to London at the expense of the Earl of Blessington, who treated her not as a mistress, but as a fiancée. The only hitch, and it was a considerable one, was Captain Maurice St Leger Farmer, aka Margaret's no-good husband. Fate, however, smiled on the couple, if not on Farmer. His fortunes had taken a turn for the disastrous and he had been sentenced to a stint in the King's Bench Prison, where he was killed when he fell from a window during a boozed-up orgy. A few months later, Margaret Farmer became the sophisticated Marguerite, Countess of Blessington.

Lord Blessington was besotted with his new wife and spoiled her rotten. The couple left the earl's unimpressed children in Ireland and revelled in London's high life as they made an opulent home in St James's Square. Yet Marguerite had reckoned without the sniffy social hierarchy in England, where even the title of Countess wasn't a guarantee of welcome. She was a commoner who had lived in sin before bagging a titled and wealthy man, and that meant she could never hope to be the equal of her social peers. Few ladies came to visit, but they had underestimated the Countess of Blessington: she had survived far worse than social isolation.

Denied the company of upper-class ladies of merit, Marguerite turned her attention elsewhere. Though the snub must have stung, she focused instead on hosting salons filled with the movers and shakers who kept the worlds of arts and politics turning. Marguerite was drawn to any field in which there were interesting people to meet and fascinating stories to tell. She was intelligent and accomplished, celebrated by some, and whispered about by others, so it was hardly a surprise when scandal came calling.

It began when Alfred, Count d'Orsay, visited the Blessingtons in 1821. Dashing, handsome and charming, he was soon a favourite of both husband and wife so, of course, society drawing rooms began to echo with accusations of adultery. There were even those who dared to suggest that the affair was between the earl and the count, or that all three were entangled in all sorts of ways, yet there is little evidence to suggest that Lord Blessington was an innocent cuckold. Indeed, the group became a devoted and inseparable trio, and when the Blessingtons travelled to Europe in 1822, they were soon joined on their adventures by the young d'Orsay.

One can well imagine the rumours that swirled around the glamorous and wealthy travellers, who were accompanied by an impressive entourage. The party was bound for Genoa and an audience with Lord Byron, whom Lady Blessington could scarcely wait to meet. Like the infamous poet, she knew what it was to have notoriety as a constant companion and just like him, she had weathered the storm. Byron and Marguerite were kindred spirits and soon after meeting, they had already formed the deep friendship that would provide the basis of her book, *Conversations of Lord Byron*. To those she had left behind in England who had judged her on her actions and found her wanting, Marguerite's latest escapade was no surprise. Indeed, when the book came out and was well-received, they even accused her of fabricating its contents to enhance her fame. Lady Blessington little concerned herself with the people who had turned their backs on her though, not when she had her adoring coterie of thinkers fluttering around her.

Byron grew so fond of Lady Blessington that he hoped she and her husband would settle in Genoa, but eventually they moved on and left the adoring poet behind. During their Grand Tour, Lady Blessington gathered stories, characters and material that would later fuel her writings, but the happy interlude was not without its tragedies. In 1823, with the party bound for Naples, the Blessingtons received word that

Luke, Lord Blessington's son and heir, was dead. The boy was only 9 years old and his death shook the earl, who left his wife in Naples to return to Ireland to tidy his affairs.

It was during this period that Lord Blessington changed his will, ostensibly to favour his beloved friend, d'Orsay. To add further fuel to the fire of gossip, in 1827, the count married Blessington's 15-year-old daughter, Lady Harriet, in accordance with a request in the earl's new will. In return for agreeing to the marriage, d'Orsay would become heir to the wealthy Blessington estates in Dublin, but from the very start, the union was a miserable one. Young Lady Harriet had never really known her mother, and she resented her father for leaving her behind as he went gadding about the continent with Marguerite. Now she was saddled with a husband that she didn't want and she blamed her stepmother entirely. Yet it was Marguerite, perhaps mindful of her own unhappy fate as a teenage bride, who stipulated that the marriage must not be consummated for four years.

The wedding between d'Orsay and Harriet seemed to mark the end of the Blessingtons' happiest days in Europe. By the time the group settled in Paris in 1828, Marguerite had begun to suffer from depression, whilst her husband was labouring under a variety of maladies. He died after suffering a stroke in 1829, aged just 46.

Lady Blessington was heartbroken, but there was worse to come. She found that her income as a widow was nowhere near enough to support the lifestyle she had enjoyed with her husband, and she was left with no choice but to return to London, where even more misfortune awaited. Mere months after the earl's death, British newspapers began to intimate that Marguerite and d'Orsay were lovers. London society lapped it up, and Marguerite found herself more alone than ever. Still, she held her salons and put on a public face that never so much as wavered. She was too proud to show how much the rumours and isolation must have hurt.

Lady Blessington's final humiliation came with the very public collapse of Harriet and d'Orsay's marriage in 1831. Harriet was happy to become the darling of Marguerite's enemies, who celebrated her as a wronged innocent who had been sucked into a family beset by vice and shamelessness. It didn't help that d'Orsay went to stay with Marguerite after the split, further fuelling the belief that she had cuckolded her own stepdaughter. In fact, Harriet was far from innocent and soon rumours about her own affairs began to spread. Those claims were dismissed as the spiteful lies of Marguerite and d'Orsay, even though they weren't responsible for them. Even when she was innocent, Lady Blessington was still regarded as the guilty party. But Marguerite was a survivor and that would never change. 'I am now an old woman,' she told a friend, 'And I have never for a moment repented the independent line of conduct I have adopted.'[2]

Count d'Orsay's extravagance and her own dwindling coffers eventually led Marguerite to take up her pen once more, and she worked tirelessly to keep the money coming in. The salons she held at Gore House became more popular than ever, but still she couldn't balance the books. Eventually, Marguerite was left with no choice but to sell her worldly possessions to pay for her debts and those of d'Orsay, who had already burned through the £100,000 he had received from his estranged wife in return for giving up his claim to the Blessington estates. The scandalous twosome took up residence in Paris, where Lady Marguerite died before the sale of the Gore House inventory was completed. Nobody mourned her more deeply than d'Orsay. 'I have lost everything in the world,' he lamented, 'for she was to me a mother, a dear mother, a true and loving mother.'[3] When he died three years later, he was laid to rest at her side.

2. Sadleir, Michael (1947). *The Strange Life of Lady Blessington*. New York: Farrar, Strauss & Giroux, p.204.
3. Molloy, Joseph Fitzgerald (1896). *The Most Gorgeous Lady Blessington, Vol II*. London: Downey & Co, p.228.

The Courtesan's Quill

In which a famed courtesan puts pen to paper…

SIR,— To travel fifty-two miles this bad weather, merely to see a man, with only the given number of legs, arms, fingers, &c., would, you must admit, be madness in a girl like myself, surrounded by humble admirers who are ever ready to travel any distance for the honour of kissing the tip of her little finger; but, if you can prove to me that you are one bit better than any man who may be ready to attend my bidding, I'll e'en start for London directly. So, if you can do anything better in the way of pleasing a lady than ordinary men, write directly: if not, adieu, Monsieur le Prince.[1]

In these pages, we have met many people who were ruined by scandal, most of them women. Yet Harriette Wilson had the skills to turn notoriety to her advantage, for she didn't fear public approbation. After all, Harriette knew that money could cushion the blow of even the most vicious gossip.

Born Harriette Dubouchet in 1786, by the time she wrote the letter above rejecting the notoriously licentious Prince of Wales, Harriette was one of the most celebrated courtesans in Britain. Along with her sister, Amy, and Julia Johnstone, Harriette was renowned in London as one of the Three Graces, and every man longed for even a fleeting taste of their favours.

Harriette had been born into respectability, but she pined for excitement and she wasn't alone. Of the fifteen children of the Dubouchet family,

---

1. Wilson, Harriette (1909). *The Memoirs of Harriette Wilson, Written by Herself, Vol I.* London: Eveleigh Nash, p.8.

four became courtesans, whilst one went as far in the other direction as might have seemed possible. As her sisters were entertaining the most celebrated men in London, young Sophia gave up her career as a courtesan to marry Baron Berwick instead.

But respectable marriage was not what Harriette wanted. At the age of 15, she became the mistress of Lord Craven, and he was just the first step in an illustrious career. She instinctively understood that part of the key to making a success of her chosen profession was the creation of a mystique, so a man couldn't simply hire Harriette Wilson. Instead, he must make a convincing case for her company, endure interviews, and prove his financial and social pulling power was suitably impressive. And as the Prince of Wales discovered, even that didn't guarantee an audience. One of Harriette's PR master strokes was how she advertised herself. She chose the men she wanted to make an arrangement with, and wrote saucy letters to them in which she invited them to make her acquaintance. Many took her up on the offer.

Unlike Mrs Armistead, whose former patrons rallied to her aid when she needed them, once Harriette's celebrity had faded, she found that none of her famed lovers wanted to know. All through her life she had served rich men and most of them had promised her a pension once the affair was over, but just as the Prince of Wales forgot his promise to Mary Robinson, so too did Harriette find that their words were worthless. Yet this was not a woman who would sit and mope on her fate. Instead, as Harriette's fortieth birthday approached, she decided that if they would not pay the promised pensions, then she would make money off those influential and supposedly respectable men another way.

If they thought she would go quietly, they were about to get a big surprise. Harriette Wilson inked her nib and began to write her memoirs, beginning with the famed line, 'I shall not say how and why I became, at the age of fifteen, the mistress of the Earl of Craven.' As opening lines go, it was one of the most sensational around.

Before Harriette's serialised memoirs went to press each week, she contacted each man featured in the forthcoming instalment and offered to remove his name for the sum of £200. Unsurprisingly, Harriette found that plenty of her former clients were keen to pay the fee and spare their blushes. It was the first modern kiss and tell, and it saved Harriette Wilson from poverty, assuring her a luxurious retirement. It also assured her rejection by polite society, but Harriette didn't care – she would hardly miss what she had never had in the first place. She was well used to life in the demi-monde, and she was perfectly happy to remain there and count her cash.

One man who refused to pay the £200 asked of him was the Duke of Wellington. He famously told Harriette to 'publish, and be damned', and she took him at his word. Harriette savaged the Iron Duke as a boring, unimaginative lover, more akin to a ratcatcher than a national hero. Of course, none of the men she named found themselves disbarred from polite society, but such was the way of the world. It's little wonder that Harriette Wilson decided to kick against it.

A Whisper of Scandal: A French Fancy

Sophie Dawes exchanged a childhood spent in the workhouse for life at the Bourbon court, as the wife of a senior royal guard. As far as her unsuspecting husband knew, Louis Henri, Prince of Condé, was Sophie's father, but in reality, he had met her in a London brothel and brought her to France as his lover. Though Sophie was banished from court once the truth came out, the prince's will assured her a payment of 10 million francs on his death. Little wonder that when Condé was found hanging by his neck from a window, every finger pointed Sophie's way. When she was eventually cleared of any involvement in the prince's death, Sophie collected her inheritance and returned to England, a far cry from the workhouse child she had once been.

The Bishop and the Guardsman

In which a man of the cloth faces ruin…

> The Devil to prove the Church was a farce
> Went out to fish for a Bugger.
> He baited the hook with a Soldier's arse
> And pulled up the Bishop of Clogher.

In 1822 a scandal erupted in the Church of Ireland so great that it led the Archbishop of Canterbury to lament that 'it was not safe for a bishop to shew himself in the streets of London'. Percy Jocelyn, the gentleman who started it, had been discovered not just in flagrante, but in flagrante in the back room of the White Lion pub in Westminster, with a half-naked Grenadier Guardsman. In a world where scandal was social currency, where an earl taking a 15-year-old as his mistress was blithely accepted so long as he showed discretion, it was the seemingly innocuous matter of consensual sex that brought down the Bishop of Clogher.

Percy Jocelyn was the third son of Robert Jocelyn, 1st Earl of Roden, whose wealth encompassed vast estates in County Down. With no hope of succeeding to the title, Percy attended Dublin's Trinity College where the lanky, scholarly, young man made little impact. Upon his graduation he followed the example of many a younger son and took holy orders, his career path cushioned and smoothed by his illustrious family name and wealth. He didn't need to be remarkable to climb the ranks, just well connected.

In 1809 Jocelyn was installed as the Bishop of Ferns and Leighlin, but he had been in office just two years when he had his first brush with scandal. James Byrne, a coachman in the employ of Jocelyn's brother, accused the Bishop of Ferns and Leighlin of 'taking indecent familiarities' with him, and of regaling him with obscene suggestions.

The outraged Jocelyn denied the allegations and sued the coachman. He won the case, and Byrne was sentenced to two years in prison and the agony of public flogging. Percy Jocelyn emerged from the affair with his name intact, free from any suspicion.

That was merely the overture to what was to come. Shortly after he was invested as Bishop of Clogher, Jocelyn arranged a fateful liaison in the White Lion. His partner was a Grenadier Guardsman named John Moverley, who was more than thirty-five years younger than the 58-year-old bishop. The two men agreed to meet after Jocelyn concluded his business in the House of Lords, and with Jocelyn in his clerical black and Moverley in his uniform, they could hardly go unnoticed.

Believing themselves to be unobserved, the pair left the public bar for a private room, little suspecting that they had aroused suspicions. James Plant, the landlord's son-in-law, crept out of the pub and peeped into the private room through a window. There he saw the two men half-naked, 'in the state of Achilles.' The landlord of the White Lion summoned the watch, who joined a growing crowd at the window to observe the encounter. Only when the men were about to consummate their arrangement – witnesses couldn't agree on whether it was Jocelyn who was about to penetrate Moverley, or vice versa – did the mob storm the room. A struggle followed and Jocelyn fought desperately to escape, leading diarist Charles Greville to note dryly, 'if his breeches had not been down they think he would have got away.'[1]

With the benefit of distance, it is easy to read such comments with humour, but one cannot overestimate the potential outcome of this affair in the nineteenth century. Both men faced ruin, criminal charges, a trial and guaranteed public humiliation, simply because of their sexuality. Sodomy was a capital offence until 1861, and the last men to be hanged on such a charge were James Pratt and John Smith, who were executed in 1835.[2] When Jocelyn and Moverley were taken to a holding cell in Vine Street, they were followed by a catcalling crowd, giving them just a taste of what they could expect to endure as the events unfolded.

Even in custody, Jocelyn refused to give his name, but his identity was discovered thanks to a letter found in his pocket. When the men

---

1. Fulford, Roger (ed.) (1963). *The Greville Memoirs*. New York: Macmillan, p.8.
2. Pratt and Smith were eventually pardoned in 2017 by the 'Alan Turing law'.

were brought before the bench the following day, both pleaded not guilty. Because they were arrested before intercourse had taken place, they could not be charged with the capital offence of sodomy, but with a misdemeanour, which meant that they could be granted bail. The Bishop of Clogher was able to post his £500 bail, much to the chagrin of the public who argued that the sum was too low for such a wealthy man. It was the last the court saw of him.

Percy Jocelyn fled for the continent then secretly made for Scotland, where he hid out under an alias. In some ways, it was a relief to the English judiciary, which can hardly have relished a trial. Few were surprised that the bishop had fled the scene, and fewer still didn't suspect that it was just what the establishment had been hoping for. Of course, Jocelyn's escape didn't help Moverley, who still languished in custody.

'The greatest dissatisfaction would pervade the publick [*sic*] mind at the escape of the Bishop and the punishment of the Soldier,' wrote Greville. 'The people, who cannot discriminate [will] see only in such apparent injustice a disposition to shield an offender in the higher classes of society from the consequences of his crimes.'[3] Years later, when magistrate Hensleigh Wedgwood wrote to the Home Secretary seeking clemency for Pratt and Smith, the last men to be executed in England for sodomy, he too commented that 'It is … the only capital crime that is committed by rich men but … they are never convicted.'

No doubt hoping to avoid the sensation of a trial and all the revelations it would entail, senior members of the government began to speculate that it might be better for all concerned if someone could bail Moverley out of prison and arrange for him to conveniently disappear too. Jocelyn's family took the bait and paid Moverley's bail. Once he was free, it came as a surprise to no one that the guardsman made good his escape. He too was never heard from again.

In the aftermath, newspapers and the public alike clamoured for justice for James Byrne, the coachman who had been flogged and imprisoned in 1811. As some called for the bishop to be hunted down and punished to the fullest extent of the law – essentially, they wanted him to hang –

---

3. Ibid.

others focused on raising money so Byrne could be compensated for his wrongful punishment. His name was cleared at last.

Percy Jocelyn, meanwhile, laid low. In his absence, he was removed from his ecclesiastical office and took domestic jobs in Scotland under an assumed name. He was the subject of bawdy jokes, ballads, caricatures and pamphlets, and his story cast a long shadow over some. Mere months after the scandal broke, Robert Stewart, the troubled and paranoid Viscount Castlereagh, told George IV that 'I am accused of the same crime as the Bishop of Clogher'. He too had gone to bed with a soldier, whom he claimed he thought was a woman in male dress. A short time later, he took his own life.

Percy Jocelyn never returned to England, but instead remained in Scotland where he worked as a butler under the name Thomas Wilson. His true identity only came to light after his death on 2 December 1843. Buried in a coffin that carried no name, the Latin inscription read, 'Here lie the remains of a great sinner, saved by grace, whose hopes rest in the atoning sacrifice of the Lord Jesus Christ'. In a final twist, however, when the Jocelyn family vault was opened, it was discovered that it contained one additional but unidentified coffin. Perhaps this was the disgraced Bishop of Clogher, incognito one last time.

A Whisper of Scandal: We Are Not Amused

Unmarried Lady Flora Hastings was rumoured to have enjoyed an affair with John Conroy, the ruthless and domineering comptroller of the household of the Duchess of Kent. The duchess just happened to be Queen Victoria's mother, who was also rumoured to be sharing her bed with Conroy. When Lady Flora visited the doctor to complain of a swollen stomach, he told her that she was pregnant. Despite Lady Flora's protestations that she couldn't be with child, the young queen castigated her, furious to have her court embroiled in such a scandal. When a second diagnosis confirmed that Lady Flora's symptoms were actually those of terminal liver cancer, the queen rushed to her bedside to make amends before it was too late.

Gentleman Jack of Shibden Hall

In which a Yorkshire businesswoman follows her own path…

I love her & her heart is mine in return. Liberty & wavering made us both wretched & why throw away our happiness so foolishly? She is my wife in honour & in love & why not acknowledge her such openly & at once? I am satisfied to have her mind, & my own, at ease.[1]

We began our romp through a century of scandal with the tale of Miss Lavinia Fenton, who enjoyed a short but celebrated career during the reign of King George I. She witnessed the beginning of the Georgian era, so it seems only appropriate that we conclude our journey with a remarkable woman who saw its end and lived through the dawning of the Victorian age. She was a trailblazer whose legacy is celebrated more than ever today.

Anne Lister was born on 3 April 1791 and divided her early years between school in Ripon and the family home of Skefler House in Market Weighton. She also made frequent trips to Halifax to visit her aunt and uncle at Shibden Hall, where she would eventually flourish. In 1806 Anne began the first volume of her famed diaries, which eventually extended to thousands of pages and were partially written in a secret code that concealed her most intimate dreams and desires. Within those pages, the woman who has become famed to modern audiences as *Gentleman Jack* hid her most private life, forging her way in a time when to live openly as a lesbian was virtually unheard of. Yet despite having to

1. Whitbread, Helena (ed.) (1992). *I Know My Own Heart*. New York: New York University Press, p.154.

hide this fundamental part of her character, Anne concealed little else. She rejected the accepted signifiers of late Georgian and early Victorian femininity, instead dressing in masculine clothes, travelling widely to indulge her love of hiking and exploring, and managing a successful industrial portfolio. It's little wonder that her story continues to inspire.

Anne's first same-sex relationships were at boarding school where she was a strong-willed and intelligent student. She began an affair with a pupil named Eliza Raine, who stood to inherit a fortune that Anne hoped would pave the way for them to lead a more independent life as adults, but this affair proved an awakening in more ways than one. Still a teen, Anne didn't want to settle for one woman just yet and hoped to indulge what she called her 'oddity' by taking other lovers and travelling widely across the continent. When Anne began to romance other girls, Eliza was left heartbroken. She never recovered from the pain of Anne's rejection and ended her days in an asylum.

Anne found love in the shape of Mariana Belcombe, the daughter of a wealthy local doctor, and the young women conducted a secret and passionate love affair in full view of their unsuspecting families. They even exchanged rings, though society thought that they were merely two women with that intimate sort of friendship that had previously been ascribed to the ladies of Llangollen. Anne had fallen in love with Mariana as surely as Eliza had fallen in love with Anne, but this time it was she who was to suffer heartbreak. In 1815, Mariana married. She asked Anne to accompany her on her honeymoon, and though Anne went along, she despaired every moment of the trip. She believed that in marrying a rich man rather than following her heart, Mariana had succumbed to a socially accepted version of prostitution. They parted ways, but Anne couldn't forget her adored Mariana.

After a brief fling with Mariana's sister, the two women were thrown together again. They had not met for a year, yet when Anne visited her former lover, the attraction between them proved too strong to resist. Anne and Mariana began an affair that lasted for years and, through it all, Mariana lived a double life as a loyal wife on the one hand and committed lover of Anne Lister on the other. Indeed, Anne considered herself to be married to Mariana in all but law, but she had reckoned without Mariana's desperation to keep up her public image as a model society wife.

Anne Lister stood out from the crowd. In her preferred garb of dark, masculine clothes, she was catcalled as she strode through Halifax, openly propositioned, and crudely asked if she was a man or woman. She suffered a host of nicknames, including the posthumous *Gentleman Jack*, and endured near-constant harassment, including a disturbing incident in which a man tried to put his hand up her skirts, claiming that it was the only way to determine whether she was truly female. Through all of it, Anne would not be cowed, and it was her irrepressible determination to be true to herself that eventually ended her relationship with Mariana.

Mariana had accepted an invitation to visit Anne at Shibden and, on the day of her expected arrival, a storm broke overhead. Anne set off walking despite the deluge, and strode 10 miles across the Yorkshire moors to intercept her lover's coach. She climbed onto the vehicle and hopped inside to greet Mariana, her sister and their maid, expecting to receive a warm welcome. Far from being delighted, Mariana was furious. It was a strange thing to do, Mariana thundered, and one that was sure to start gossip about them. A short time later, Mariana told Anne that she could no longer bear to be seen in public with her. What she called Anne's 'masculine' appearance had become an embarrassment to her.

It was a familiar story for Anne Lister. She had numerous affairs with women, all of whom went to pains to conceal them. This was an era in which lesbianism was barely even acknowledged; it was not included in legislation banning homosexuality, simply because it was not thought of as prevalent enough to require legal intervention. Yet Anne's sex life was full and rich and it spanned the continent. It was a fundamental part of her character and it meant that her heart was broken more than once. She had hoped to make a wife of Vere Hobart, sister of the 5th Earl of Buckinghamshire, but after a whirlwind trip to France, Vere too elected to marry a man. It was another hard knock.

Business was also fundamental to Anne Lister's life, not least because her wide-ranging European travels had brought her to the brink of financial ruin. She revitalised the fading splendour of Shibden Hall by injecting cash into the estate's coal mines, extending them and growing their income considerably. In an era where women were not expected to be business leaders, Anne once again bucked the trend. She went up against her male peers and soon proved that she was a formidable opponent. There were few estate managers so dedicated as Anne Lister, and her interests thrived. Once she had travelled Europe to escape the boredom and stifling walls of Shibden, but now it was the place in which she was to discover her greatest happiness.

Years earlier, Anne had met a younger woman named Ann Walker, the shy daughter of a neighbouring estate owner. Miss Walker had made little impact on her forthright neighbour, but when the two women met again as Ann approached the age of 30, that changed. Anne Lister was enchanted by her neighbour, and not a little attracted by the fortune she stood to inherit too. Happily, Ann Walker was more than keen to return the sentiment and soon the women were in love. For Ann Walker, whose fiancé had recently died, a little bit of adoration was just the balm she needed.

When Anne suggested that they live together at Shibden Hall as though they were a married couple, the younger woman was understandably hesitant to make such a commitment. She feared the rejection of society and asked her lover to give her thinking time. Anne did just that and once again took off for Europe. When she returned, she found that Ann Walker had made up her mind. She had rejected a male suitor's advances and was ready to commit herself fully to Anne Lister.

On Easter Sunday in 1834, the two women took communion together at the Holy Trinity Church in Goodramgate, York, and exchanged rings. Theirs has become recognised as the first lesbian marriage in Britain and is one of the many elements of Anne Lister's life that have led some to refer to her as the first modern lesbian. After the communion, the tide of gossip swept once more towards *Gentleman Jack*, and anonymous letters arrived at Shibden Hall mocking the marriage. Someone even paid to place a facetious advertisement in the *Leeds Mercury* that scoffed at the marriage of *Captain Tom Lister* and Ann Walker. Yet the women faced this with extraordinary strength of character and will. They left the small minds to think what they would, and embarked on an extended honeymoon.

For the rest of Anne's life, she and her wife lived together at Shibden Hall. They travelled widely and undertook their last trip in 1839, touring through France, Denmark and Sweden, before reaching Russia in the freezing depths of winter. As they journeyed on through Eastern Europe, Anne suffered an insect bite that turned septic. She died of fever on 22 September 1840 at Kutaisi in Georgia. Grief-stricken, Ann Walker returned to England where she languished in solitude. Anne had willed Shibden Hall and its estate to her wife, and the grieving widow locked herself away behind its walls. When the concerned Walker family convinced a police officer to break the door down, they found the house in disarray and Ann in a state of utter despair, a loaded pistol at her side.

Ann Walker joined Eliza Raine in the asylum. Ironically, one of the physicians who cared for her was the father of Mariana Belcombe, the first woman to break Anne Lister's heart. It was a tragic end to a singular love story.

The rediscovery and subsequent decoding of Anne Lister's diaries has allowed modern readers to learn for the first time the true story of a woman who broke the mould. Anne was single-minded, dedicated and driven, a woman of extraordinary intelligence and will. It would have taken more than sneering catcalls in the street to stop her from pursuing her business, or her lovers. She has become a modern icon, remembered as the trailblazer she truly was.

Afterword

Bare innocence is no support
When you are tried in Scandal's court.[1]

And so, as the carriages arrive to carry the ton home to their opulent houses and grand estates, Lady Whistledown can once again open her inkpot and prime her pen, safe in the knowledge that there will be more than enough scandal to fill her gossip pamphlets for years to come. It has been said that life can be stranger than fiction, and amongst the Georgian upper classes, it could certainly be more vicious. Ruin lurked around every corner and, in a world where every action was scrutinised and used as social currency, it didn't pay to let one's guard down for a moment.

Today, perhaps, we would like to think that we are a little more forgiving, and certainly more open-minded. In many ways that's true, but in others, the price of notoriety can be as high in the twenty-first century as it was for the Georgians. The antics of the Prince Regent may no longer fill the gossip columns, but there are more than enough infamous names just waiting to pick up the baton where he left it.

1. Swift, Jonathan (1823). *The Select Works of Jonathan Swift, Vol. IV.* London: Hector McLean, p.207.

Bibliography

Aldrich, Robert, & Wotherspoon, Garry. *Who's Who in Gay & Lesbian History*. Abingdon-on-Thames: Taylor & Francis, 2020.

Alexander, Boyd (ed.). *Life at Fonthill, 1807–1822*. London: Rupert Hart-Davis Ltd, 1957.

Andrew, Donna T. *Aristocratic Vice*. New Haven: Yale University Press, 2013.

Anonymous. *An Authentic Detail of Particulars Relative to the Late Duchess of Kingston*. London: G. Kearsley, 1788.

Anonymous. *Copies of the Depositions of the Witnesses Examined in the Cause of Divorce Now Depending in the Consistory Court of the Lord Bishop of London, at Doctor's-Commons*. London: J. Russell, 1771.

Anonymous. *Correspondence of Horace Walpole with George Montague, Esq, Vol III*. London: Henry Colburn, 1837.

Anonymous. *Four Genuine Letters, Which Lately Passed Between a Noble Lord, and a Young Woman of Fashion*. London: Matthew Williamson, 1762.

Anonymous. *Fraser's Magazine for Town and Country, Vol LII*. London: John W. Parker and Son, 1855.

Anonymous. *A Full and Complete History of His R—l H—ss the D— of C—d, and Lady G—r, the Fair Adulteress, Vol I*. London: J. Porter and T. Walker, 1770.

Anonymous. *The Hibernian Magazine, or Compendium of Entertaining Knowledge, Vol V*. Dublin: Thomas Walker, 1775.

Anonymous. *Journals of the House of Lords, Vol. L*. London: His Majesty's Stationery Office, 1814.

Anonymous. *The Lawyer's and Magistrate's Magazine, Vol III for the Year MDCCXCI*. London: W. Jones, 1794.

Anonymous. *The Letters of Lord Nelson to Lady Hamilton, Vol I*. London: Thomas Lovewell & Co, 1814.

Anonymous. *The Letters of the Celebrated Junius, Vol I*. London: Privately published, 1783.

Anonymous. *The Life and Memoirs of Elizabeth Chudleigh, Afterwards Mrs Hervey and Countess of Bristol*. London: R. Randall, 1788.

Anonymous. *The Life of Lavinia Beswick, Alias Fenton, Alias Polly Peachum*. London: A. Moore, 1728.

Anonymous. *Love at First Sight; Or, the History of Miss Caroline Stanhope*. London: Privately published, 1773.

Anonymous. *Nocturnal Revels, Vol II*, London: M. Goadby, 1779.

Anonymous. *Notes and Queries, Six Series, Volume First*. London: John Francis, 1880.

Anonymous. *The Rocks of Meillerie*. London: R. Faulder, 1780.

Anonymous. *The Scots Magazine, and Edinburgh Literary Miscellany, Vol. LXXVI*. Edinburgh: Archibald Constable and Company, 1814.

Anonymous. *The Town and Country Magazine, or Universal Repository of Knowledge, Instruction, and Entertainment*. London: A. Hamilton Jnr, 1771.

Anonymous. *The Town and Country Magazine, or Universal Repository of Knowledge, Instruction, and Entertainment, Vol II for the Year 1770*. London: A. Hamilton Jnr, 1770.

Anonymous. *The Town and Country Magazine, or Universal Repository of Knowledge, Instruction, and Entertainment, Vol VII for the Year 1775*. London: A. Hamilton Jnr, 1775.

Anonymous. *The Trial of Mrs Biscoe, for Adultery with Robert Gordon, Esq*. London: Allen and West, 1794.

Anonymous. *The Trial of Sir Henry Mildmay, Bart*. London: R. Butters, 1814.

Anonymous. *Trials for Adultery: Or, The History of Divorces, Vol I*. London: S. Bladon, 1779.

Baildon, W. Paley (ed.). *The Home Counties Magazine*. London: Reynell & Son, 1899.

Baker, Kenneth (2005). 'George IV: A Sketch'. *History Today*. 55 (10): pp.30–36.

Barker, Hannah, and Chalus, Elaine (eds.). *Gender in Eighteenth-Century England*. London: Routledge, 1997.

Bell, Eva Mary (ed.). *The Hamwood Papers of the Ladies of Llangollen and Caroline Hamilton*. London: Macmillan and Company, 1930.

Black, Jeremy. *The Hanoverians: The History of a Dynasty*. London: Hambledon and London, 2007.

Bleackley, Horace. *Casanova in England*. London: John Lane, 1923.

Blessington, Marguerite, Countess of. *Conversations of Lord Byron with the Countess of Blessington*. Philadelphia: E.L. Carey & A. Hart, 1836.

Bryson, Bill. *At Home*. London: Transworld, 2010.

Colquhoun, Patrick. *Treatise on the Wealth, Power and Resources of the British Empire*. London: Joseph Mawman, 1814.

Cox, Millard. *Derby: The Life and Times of the 12th Earl of Derby*. London: J.A. Allan, 1974.

Cruikshank, Dan. *The Secret History of Georgian London*. London: Random House, 2010.

Cunningham, Peter (ed.). *The Letters of Horace Walpole, Earl of Orford, Vol VI*. London: Henry G. Bohn, 1861.

Cunningham, Peter (ed.). *The Letters of Horace Walpole, Earl of Orford, Vol IX*. London: Henry G. Bohn, 1859.

Curling, Jonathan. *Edward Wortley Montagu: The Man in the Iron Wig*. London: Andrew Melrose, 1954.

David, Saul. *Prince of Pleasure*. New York: Grove Press, 2000.

Davis, I.M. *The Harlot and the Statesman*. Windsor: The Kensal Press, 1986.

Derry, John W. *Charles James Fox*. New York: St. Martin's Press, 1972.

Dickson, Leigh Wetherall. 'The Construction of a Reputation for Madness: The Case Study of Lady Caroline Lamb.' *Working with English: Medieval and Modern Language, Literature and Drama*, vol. 2, University of Nottingham, 2005–2006, pp.27–46.

Dobson, Austin. *Horace Walpole: A Memoir*. New York: Dodd, Mead and Company, 1893.

Doran, John. *A Lady of the Last Century*. London: Richard Bentley and Son, 1873.

Douglass, Paul. *The Whole Disgraceful Truth*. London: Palgrave Macmillan, 2006.

Douglass, Paul, & March, Rosemary. 'That "Vital Spark of Genius": Lady Caroline Lamb's Writing before Byron.' *Pacific Coast Philology*, vol. 41, Penn State University Press, 2006, pp.43–62, http://www.jstor.org/stable/25474199.

Erskine, Beatrice. *Lady Diana Beauclerk, Her Life and Work*. London: Thomas Fisher Unwin, 1903.

Fox, Henry, & Fox-Strangeways, Stephen, Earl of Ilchester. *Letters to Henry Fox, Lord Holland, With a Few Addressed to His Brother, Stephen, Earl of Ilchester*. London: The Roxburgh Club, 1915.

Fulford, Roger (ed.). *The Greville Memoirs*. New York: Macmillan, 1963.

Fyvie, John. *Comedy Queens of the Georgian Era*. New York: E.P. Dutton and Company, 1907.

Gervat, Claire. *Elizabeth: The Scandalous Life of the Duchess of Kingston*. London: Arrow Books, 2004.

Gordon, Pryse Lockhart. *Personal Memoirs or Reminiscences of Men and Manners at Home and Abroad, Vol II*. London: Henry Colburn and Richard Bentley, 1830.

Hampl, Patricia. *The Art of the Wasted Day*. London: Penguin Books, 2019.

Hawkesworth, John (ed.). *Letters, Written by the Late Jonathan Swift, DD*. London: T. Davies, 1766.

Herbert, Baron Sidney Charles (ed.). *The Pembroke Papers*. London: Jonathan Cape, 1950.

Hicklin, John. *The Ladies of Llangollen*. Chester: Thomas Catherall, 1847.

Hickman, Katie. *Courtesans*. London: Harper Collins, 2003.

Hicks, Carola. *Improper Pursuits: The Scandalous Life of an Earlier Lady Diana Spencer*. New York: St Martin's Press, 2002.

Highfill, Philip H., Burnim, Kalman A., and Langhans, Edward A. *A Biographical Dictionary of Actresses, Musicians, Dancers, Managers & Other Stage Personnel in London, 1660–1800*. Carbondale: Southern Illinois University Press, 1993.

Hilton, Boyd. *A Mad, Bad & Dangerous People?*. Oxford: Clarendon Press, 2006.

Hinde, Thomas. *Courtiers: 900 Years of Court Life*. London: Victor Gollancz, 1986.

Hyde, H. Montgomery. *A Tangled Web*. London: Constable, 1986.

Inglis, Lucy. *Georgian London: Into the Streets*. London: Penguin, 2013.

Jeaffreson, John Cordy. *Lady Hamilton and Lord Nelson, Vol. II*. London: Hurst and Blackett, Limited, 1888.

Jesse, John Heneage. *George Selwyn and His Contemporaries, Vol II*. London: Richard Bentley, 1843.

Lacey, Brian. *Terrible Queer Creatures*. Dublin: Wordwell Ltd, 2019.

Law, Susan C. *Through the Keyhole*. Stroud: The History Press, 2015.

Leslie, Charles Robert, and Taylor, Tom. *Life and Times of Sir Joshua Reynolds, Vol I*. London: John Murray, 1865.

L'Estrange, A.G. *The Life of Mary Russell Mitford, Vol. I*. London: Richard Bentley, 1870.

Leveson-Gower, F. (ed.). *Letters of Harriet Countess Granville, Vol I*. London: Longmans, Green, and Co, 1894.

Levy, Martin. *Love and Madness*. London: HarperCollins, 2009.

Lewis, W.S., and Smith, Robert A. *Horace Walpole's Correspondence*. New Haven: Yale University Press, 1961.

Linnane, Fergus. *Madams, Bawds and Brothel Keepers of London*. Stroud: Sutton Publishing, 2005.

Longman, Charles James. *Longman's Magazine, Vol XLVI*. Longmans, Green, and Co, 1905.

Lord, Evelyn. *The Hell-Fire Clubs*. New Haven: Yale University Library, 2008.

McCormick, Donald. *The Hell-Fire Club*. London: Jarrolds, 1958.

McLaren, Angus. *Impotence: A Cultural History*. Chicago: University of Chicago Press, 2007.

Matoff, Susan. *Marguerite, Countess of Blessington*. Delaware: University of Delaware Press, 2016.

Matthew, H.C.G. & Harrison, Brian. *Oxford Dictionary of National Biography, Volume 4*. Oxford: Oxford University Press, 2004.

Melville, Lewis. *Stage Favourites of the Eighteenth Century*. London: Hutchinson & Co, 1900.

Molloy, Joseph Fitzgerald. *The Most Gorgeous Lady Blessington, Vol II*. London: Downey & Co, 1896.

Morison, Stanley. *The History of the Times: 'The Thunderer' in the Making, 1785–1841*. London: *The Times*, 1935.

Norton, Rictor. *Mother Clap's Molly House*. London: Gay Men's Press, 1992.

Ostler, Catherine. *The Duchess Countess*. London: Simon & Schuster UK, 2021.

Parris, Matthew. *The Great Unfrocked*. London: Robson Books Ltd, 1998.

Pearce, Charles E. *The Amazing Duchess, Vol I*. London: Stanley Paul & Co, 1911.

Pearce, Charles E. *Polly Peachum*. New York: Brentano's, 1913.

Pigott, Charles. *The Female Jockey Club*. London: D.I. Eaton, 1794.

Pigott, Charles. *The Jockey Club*. London: H.D. Symons, 1792.

Pritchard, John. *An Account of the Ladies of Llangollen*. H. Jones: Llangollen, 1876.

Rendell, Mike. *In Bed with the Georgians*. Barnsley: Pen & Sword Books, 2018.

Riley, John C. *The Age of Horace Walpole in Caricature*. New Haven: Yale University Library, 1973.

Roberts, Geraldine. *The Angel and the Cad*. London: Picador, 2015.

Rubenhold, Hallie. *The Lady in Red*. New York: St Martin's Press, 2009.

Russell, Jack. *Nelson and the Hamiltons*. New York: Simon and Schuster, 1969.

Sadleir, Michael. *The Strange Life of Lady Blessington*. New York: Farrar, Strauss & Giroux, 1947.

Smith, E.A. *George IV*. New Haven: Yale University Press, 1999.

Stephenson, Raymond. *The Yard of Wit*. Philadelphia: University of Pennsylvania Press, 2004.

Stokes, Hugh. *The Devonshire House Circle*. London: Herbert Jenkins Limited, 1917.

Stone, Lawrence. *Broken Lives*. Oxford: Oxford University Press, 1993.

Swift, Jonathan. *The Select Works of Jonathan Swift, Vol. IV*. London: Hector McLean, 1823.

Walpole, Horace. *Letters of Horace Walpole, Earl of Orford, to Sir Horace Mann, Vol I*. London: Richard Bentley, 1843.

Walpole, Horace. *Letters of Horace Walpole, Earl of Orford, to Sir Horace Mann, Vol II*. Philadelphia: Lea & Blanchard, 1844.

Walpole, Horace. *Private Correspondence of Horace Walpole, Vol I*. London: Henry Colburn, 1837.

Whitbread, Helena (ed.). *I Know My Own Heart*. New York: New York University Press, 1992.

White, Barbara. *Queen of the Courtesans: Fanny Murray*. Stroud: The History Press, 2014.

Wilson, Frances. *The Courtesan's Revenge*. London: Faber & Faber, 2014.

Wilson, Harriette. *The Memoirs of Harriette Wilson, Written by Herself, Vol I.* London: Eveleigh Nash, 1909.

Wilson, Harriette. *The Memoirs of Harriette Wilson, Written by Herself, Vol II.* London: Eveleigh Nash, 1909.

Newspapers

All newspaper clippings are reproduced © The British Library Board; in addition to those cited, innumerable newspapers were consulted.

Websites Consulted

British History Online (https://www.british-history.ac.uk)

British Library Newspapers (https://www.gale.com/intl/primary-sources/british-library-newspapers)

Gay History and Literature by Rictor Norton (https://rictornorton.co.uk)

Georgian Papers Online (https://gpp.royalcollection.org.uk)

Hansard (http://hansard.millbanksystems.com/index.html)

Historical Texts (http://historicaltexts.jisc.ac.uk)

House of Commons Parliamentary Papers (https://archives.parliament.uk/online-resources/parliamentary-papers/)

JSTOR (www.jstor.org)

The National Archives (http://www.nationalarchives.gov.uk)

Old Bailey Proceedings Online (www.oldbaileyonline.org)

Oxford Dictionary of National Biography (http://www.oxforddnb.com)

Queen Victoria's Journals (http://www.queenvictoriasjournals.org)

State Papers Online (https://www.gale.com/intl/primary-sources/state-papers-online)

The Times Archive (http://www.thetimes.co.uk/archive)

Index